PEAR TREE POINT SCHOOL
90 Pear Tree Point Road
Darien, CT 06820
TEL: 203-655-0030

The French Revolution

Titles in the World History Series

The French Revolution

by
Phyllis Corzine

Lucent Books, P.O. Box 289011, San Diego, CA 92198-9011

Library of Congress Cataloging-in-Publication Data

Corzine, Phyllis A., 1943-
    The French Revolution / by Phyllis A. Corzine.
        p. cm.—(World History series)
    Includes bibliographical references and index.
    ISBN 1-56006-248-7
    1. France—History—Revolution, 1789-1799—Juvenile
literature.   I. Title.   II. Series.
DC148.C76   1995
944.04—dc20   94-27266
                                                  CIP
                                                   AC

Copyright 1995 by Lucent Books, Inc., P.O. Box 289011,
San Diego, California, 92198-9011

Printed in the U.S.A.

Contents

Foreword

Each year on the first day of school, nearly every history teacher faces the task of explaining why his or her students should study history. One logical answer to this question is that exploring what happened in our past explains how the things we often take for granted—our customs, ideas, and institutions—came to be. As statesman and historian Winston Churchill put it, "Every nation or group of nations has its own tale to tell. Knowledge of the trials and struggles is necessary to all who would comprehend the problems, perils, challenges, and opportunities which confront us today." Thus, a study of history puts modern ideas and institutions in perspective. For example, though the founders of the United States were talented and creative thinkers, they clearly did not invent the concept of democracy. Instead, they adapted some democratic ideas that had originated in ancient Greece and with which the Romans, the British, and others had experimented. An exploration of these cultures, then, reveals their very real connection to us through institutions that continue to shape our daily lives.

Another reason often given for studying history is the idea that lessons exist in the past from which contemporary societies can benefit and learn. This idea, although controversial, has always been an intriguing one for historians. Those who agree that society can benefit from the past often quote philosopher George Santayana's famous statement, "Those who cannot remember the past are condemned to repeat it." Historians who ascribe to Santayana's philosophy believe that, for example, studying the events that led up to the major world wars or other significant historical events would allow society to chart a different and more favorable course in the future.

Just as difficult as convincing students to realize the importance of studying history is the search for useful and interesting supplementary materials that present historical events in a context that can be easily understood. The volumes in Lucent Books' World History Series attempt to present a broad, balanced, and penetrating view of the march of history. Ancient Egypt's important wars and rulers, for example, are presented against the rich and colorful backdrop of Egyptian religious, social, and cultural developments. The series engages the reader by enhancing historical events with these cultural contexts. For example, in *Ancient Greece*, the text covers the role of women in that society. Slavery is discussed in *The Roman Empire*, as well as how slaves earned their freedom. The numerous and varied aspects of everyday life in these and other societies are explored in each volume of the series. Additionally, the series covers the major political, cultural, and philosophical ideas as the torch of civilization is passed from ancient Mesopotamia and Egypt, through Greece, Rome, Medieval Europe, and other world cultures, to the modern day.

The material in the series is formatted in a thorough, precise, and organized manner. Each volume offers the reader a comprehensive and clearly written overview of an important historical event or period. The topic under discussion is placed in a broad, historical context. For example, *The Italian Renaissance* begins with a discussion of the High Middle Ages and the loss of central control that allowed certain Italian cities to develop artistically. The book ends by looking forward to the Reformation and interpreting the societal changes that grew out of the Renaissance. Thus, students are not only involved in an historical era, but also enveloped by the events leading up to that era and the events following it.

One important and unique feature in the World History Series is the primary and secondary source quotations that richly supplement each volume. These quotes are useful in a number of ways. First, they allow students access to sources they would not normally be exposed to because of the difficulty and obscurity of the original source. The quotations range from interesting anecdotes to far-sighted cultural perspectives and are drawn from historical witnesses both past and present. Second, the quotes demonstrate how and where historians themselves derive their information on the past as they strive to reach a consensus on historical events. Lastly, all of the quotes are footnoted, familiarizing students with the citation process and allowing them to verify quotes and/or look up the original source if the quote piques their interest.

Finally, the books in the World History Series provide a detailed launching point for further research. Each book contains a bibliography specifically geared toward student research. A second, annotated bibliography introduces students to all the sources the author consulted when compiling the book. A chronology of important dates gives students an overview, at a glance, of the topic covered. Where applicable, a glossary of terms is included.

In short, the series is designed not only to acquaint readers with the basics of history, but also to make them aware that their lives are a part of an ongoing human saga. Perhaps they will then come to the same realization as famed historian Arnold Toynbee. In his monumental work, *A Study of History*, he wrote about becoming aware of history flowing through him in a mighty current, and of his own life "welling like a wave in the flow of this vast tide."

Important Dates in the History of the French Revolution

1788	1789	1790	1791	1792	1793

1788

May—King dismisses *parlements*

May-September—Revolt of nobility

Summer—Poor harvest; bread prices soar; unemployment grows

September—King agrees to call Estates General

December—King agrees Third Estate will have twice as many representatives as other two orders

1789

May 5—Estates General meet

June 17—Third Estate adopts name of "National Assembly"

June 20—Tennis Court Oath

July 11—King dismisses Necker

July 12-14—Riots in Paris

July 14—Storming of the Bastille

July-August—The Great Fear

August 4—Feudal rights abolished by National Assembly

August 26—Declaration of the Rights of Man and of the Citizen

October 5—Market-women's march to Versailles

October 6—Royal family brought to Paris

November 2—Church property confiscated

1790

Throughout the year National Assembly works on drafting the constitution

February 13—Religious orders of monks, priests, and nuns suppressed

July 12—Civil Constitution of the Clergy adopted

July 14—First Festival of the Federation

November 27—Decree ordering clergy to take oath supporting Civil Constitition of the Clergy

Fall and Winter—Growing unrest sparked by Civil Constitution of the Clergy

1791

Émigrés continue to leave France; European hostility toward Revolution grows

June 20—Royal family's flight to Varennes

July 17—Massacre at Champ de Mars

August 27—Declaration of Pillnitz

September 14—King accepts new constitution

October 1—Legislative Assembly meets for the first time

Fall and Winter—Girondins rise to power

1792

April 20—France declares war on Austria

Spring—Army meets disastrous defeats; economic situation worsens; sansculotte grow more dissatisfied

June 20—Mob invades the Tuileries

July 11—Assembly decrees *"La patrie est en danger!"*

July 25-30—*Fédérés* arrive in Paris

August 3—Paris sections petition for removal of king

August 9—Paris Insurrectionary Committee formed

August 10—The Tuileries attacked; king overthrown

September 2—Verdun falls to Prussians

September 2-6—September Massacres

September 21—First meeting of National Convention; monarchy abolished; convention declares September 22 first day of Year I of the Republic

Fall—Growing tension between Girondins and radical Jacobins; French army achieves victories

December—King Louis XVI brought to trial

1793
January 21—King Louis XVI executed
February 1—War declared on England and Holland
March 7—War declared on Spain
March 9—Convention authorizes recruitment of 300,000 men for the army
March 11—Revolt in the Vendée begins
March 21—Watch committees established
March 26—Committee of Public Safety established
April 4—General Dumouriez deserts to Austrians
May 28—Sansculotte establish insurrectionary committee in Paris
May 29-June 2—Girondins overthrown
June 24—Constitution of 1793 extends vote to all males
July 13—Marat murdered
July 27—Robespierre joins Committee of Public Safety
August 23—*Levée en masse* declared
September 5—Hebertist uprising; Terror declared
September 17—Law of Suspects

September 29—Maximum prices set
October 16—Marie Antoinette executed
October 31—Girondin leaders executed
November 8—Madame Roland executed

1794
March 24—Execution of Hebertists
April 5—Execution of Danton and followers
June 8—Festival of Supreme Being
June 10—Law of 22 *Prairial* broadens powers of the Reign of Terror to arrest "suspects"
July 28—Execution of Robespierre and followers; repeal of Law of 22 *Prairial*
July 31-August 10—Reorganization of Committee of Public Safety and Revolutionary Tribunal
Fall—"Gilded youths" attack leftists; Jacobin Club closed
December—Some Girondins return to convention

1795
April-May—Uprisings of sansculotte in Paris

May-June—The White Terror
August 22—Constitution of Year III passed
October 6—The last sansculotte uprising stopped by "whiff of grapeshot"
October 26—Directory takes power

1796
Spring—Napoléon begins Italian campaign that lasts through 1797

1797
May 27—Babeuf and conspirators executed

1798
May 18—Napoléon sails for Egypt

1799
November 9-10—Napoléon overthrows Directory, becomes first consul

The Best of Times, the Worst of Times

The French Revolution, like many revolutions, began on a tide of high hopes. It seemed at last that the ideals of the Enlightenment would be achieved: An ideal society based on reason and justice seemed a real possibility. Enlightened thinkers throughout Europe, and in America as well, watched hopefully. The Revolution, they hoped, would abolish social injustice, ignorance, and superstition. Soon human beings would live in the light of liberty, equality, and brotherhood.

The Revolution, however, degenerated into a fierce struggle among factions— each one intent on imposing its vision of the ideal society on the French people. Some revolutionary leaders were genuinely concerned with establishing a free and just society; others were cruel and ambitious men seeking to achieve power and glory for themselves. As the Revolution wore on, hopes for a new era were washed away in the terrible bloodbath of the 1792 September Massacre in which nearly fifteen hundred men, women, and children were brutally murdered. Just a few short months later, all of Europe watched in horror as the Reign of Terror began, a time when fear and the guillotine ruled the land.

The French Revolution brought more than bloodshed to France, but most people think first of the thousands, like these men, who were carted away and executed by guillotine.

Still, blood and terror were by no means the lasting legacy of the Revolution. Out of the turmoil came some fundamental changes in French society: the absolute monarchy fell; the ancien régime, the social and economic order based on feudal rights, was destroyed; the privileges of the aristocracy were destroyed; peasants were freed from feudal obligations to manor lords and to the church as well. Finally, the Revolution marked the transition from feudalism to capitalism, paving the way for the modern state.

For the most liberal French revolutionaries, however, equality was the most important and lasting principle, even though that dream was not fully realized by the end of the Revolution. Nevertheless, they recognized that liberty without equality would benefit only the privileged few. As one member of the National Convention declared in 1793, "Freedom is only a hollow sham when one class of men can starve another with impunity."[1] Holding firmly to their ideals of liberty and equality for all people, French revolutionaries proclaimed the universality of those ideals—all human beings, not just the French people, have basic rights that must be acknowledged by their governments.

The revolutionaries' insistence on equality and the universality of their claims frightened the aristocracy and many of the middle-class citizens of France as well as people in other European countries, but it united like-minded people around the world, making the French Revolution a central event in modern history. As one historian observes:

The Revolution was a world event and not merely an episode, however important, in the history of France. Before 1789 the statesmen of the great Powers had occasionally had to deal with peasant revolts or outbreaks of urban rioting but not with revolutionary movements in the modern sense. Henceforth the threat was always present to their imaginations and some-

The symbolic figure of liberty. Liberty and equality were what the French revolutionaries hoped to achieve, and in the process they spawned a worldwide movement.

times outside their windows. The French revolutionaries appealed, not to the rights of a particular past, but to universal principles they believed common to all men. . . . As legend, symbol and myth, the French Revolution was the affair of everyone.[2]

The dramatic upheavals of the Revolution touched not only French society but affected societies throughout the Western world. Although two hundred years have passed since that remarkable series of events known as the French Revolution, liberty and equality remain the ideals of democratic societies around the world.

1 Roots of Revolution

On August 23, 1754, a courier set off from the grand palace at Versailles, France, to deliver a message to King Louis XV at his palace at Choisy. The courier's mission was to announce the birth of the king's new grandson, Louis Augustus. But the courier never delivered his message. On the way, he was thrown from his horse and died of a broken neck. It was an omen, perhaps, of the terrible fate that awaited the royal child, who would grow up to become King Louis XVI.

The Divine Right of Kings

When Louis Augustus took the throne of France as King Louis XVI in 1774, one of a long line of Bourbon kings, he believed he had inherited the throne by a God-given right. This belief was called the divine right of kings, an idea held by many European people and their monarchs. According to this idea, kings received their right to rule directly from God rather than from the wishes of the people. Since God chose the king, the king had to answer only to God, not to the people—an idea that led to many abuses.

The notion of the divine right of kings had reached its height in France under Louis's great-grandfather, Louis XIV. Known as the Grand Monarch, or the Sun King, Louis XIV had ruled for seventy-two years, until 1715. He was an absolute monarch who believed he and he alone held the power of the state. "I *am* the State!" he is said to have declared. His rule was marked by despotism, extravagant

Louis XIV began the tradition of heavily taxing the lower classes and using the courts to impose his tyrannical laws upon the people.

spending, costly wars, and heavy taxation of the lower classes. Under him, the courts—instead of dispensing justice—became instruments of oppression.

His successor was little better. Louis XV was weak and pleasure loving. His mistresses and court favorites had shamelessly looted the treasury. Louis XV earned the people's hatred because of his personal extravagances and because of his costly and disastrous wars, including the Seven Years' War in which France lost its colonies in Canada and India to Great Britain. Louis XV realized that he was leaving his country in a terrible financial crisis, but he cared little. "After me, the deluge," he remarked cynically.

Louis XV used his position to indulge his extravagant whims. He cared little about the poor condition of the country after his reign.

Louis XVI and Marie Antoinette

Unlike his grandfather, Louis XVI was kindhearted and well meaning, even though he gave the appearance of coldness and formality. A high official of the court reported that he had

> never known anyone whose character was more contradicted by outward appearances. [According to this man, no one] could speak to [Louis] of disasters or accidents to people without seeing a look of compassion come over his face, yet his replies [were] often hard, his tone harsh, his manner unfeeling.[3]

Unfortunately, Louis did not have the will nor the brainpower to match his good intentions.

According to reports, Louis was an unattractive man, about five and a half feet tall and somewhat overweight. Although he had clear blue eyes and thick, fair hair, he was pale, with a full, flabby mouth and a double chin, and so nearsighted he could not recognize people more than a few feet away.

While Louis XVI was loved by many of the French at the beginning of his reign, his wife and queen, Marie Antoinette, was generally hated. She and Louis were married when he was fifteen years old and she fourteen. She was the daughter of the powerful Empress Maria-Theresa of Austria. Because Austria was a traditional enemy of France, Marie Antoinette was often referred to contemptuously as "the Austrian woman." Marie Antoinette was quick-witted, vivacious, and beautiful, with a lovely complexion, blue eyes, and fair hair. She was also an energetic woman: "I must have bustle; I must have endless change," she claimed.[4] She filled her time with

King Louis and the Hunt

Louis XVI was an avid hunter, and as Vincent Cronin reports in the biography Louis and Antoinette, *Louis's habits surrounding the hunt give some insight into his character.*

"Louis's favorite occupation was hunting the stag. He never lost an occasion of putting on the blue and crimson velvet-cuffed jacket of the King's hunt, and he found intense enjoyment in the clean smell of horses, leather and autumn leaves, the barking of the English hounds, the finding of hoof-prints . . . the growing excitement as the stag was overtaken, and then the kill. Sometimes Louis arrived alone on the scene; then he jumped down and, avoiding the antlers that could easily maim, himself plunged a hunting knife into the stag's neck.

Once in the saddle Louis threw aside the caution he showed at his desk. According to the Spanish ambassador, 'He rides so well that it is hard to follow him—indeed, it is thought that he exposes himself to dangerous falls.' Physical courage in the open air came easily to Louis; moral courage towards people he was to find more difficult.

Louis entered in his diary the result of each day's hunt, and if it was particularly eventful, wrote a detailed account of it: purely factual with no ripple of emotion. He noted the parts of the forest where stags abounded, and those where they were scarce. At the end of each year he summarized the number of stags, deer, roebuck and wild boar that had been taken. Similarly he totted up, by month and year, the number of game-birds he shot. Louis seems to have felt a need to reduce any disorder in daily life to the order of statistics. The trouble is that he made of this commendable practice a fetish. For example, at the end of each year he calculated the number of days he had spent away from Versailles, and even, when he married, the total time he had so far spent away from Versailles: 852 days. Such laboriously compiled statistics seem to have been quite useless: they suggest a tendency in Louis, at this age, to retreat from central realities to reassuring details."

Although more compassionate toward the unfortunate than were his predecessors, Louis XVI was a weak leader.

ops, to the wealthy abbots—the heads of communities of monks. Catholicism was the dominant religion in France. Although there were only about a hundred thousand members of the clergy in France during the 1700s, the church owned over 10 percent of the land, and the First Estate wielded great power in the affairs of France.

The Second Estate included the aristocrats, or nobility. Like members of the First Estate, not all aristocrats were wealthy. Although a mark of nobility was not having to work for a living, many aristocrats were farmers who worked the land themselves and lived in modest farmhouses. Heritage, or ancestry, and values determined nobility. If a person's parents belonged to the aristocracy, then that person, too, was an

flamboyant and costly activities: gambling, staging dramatic productions in which she acted a part, buying three or four new dresses every week. But her loving husband continually indulged her, refusing to deny her anything even though her activities were adding to the financial crisis in the nation.

The Three Estates

When Louis XVI took the throne, he inherited a social and political system that has since become known as the ancien régime, an ancient hierarchical system developed over centuries. Under this system, society was divided into three main groups, known as orders or estates.

The First Estate consisted of all the clergy, from the simple curés, or parish priests, to the rich and powerful archbish-

Marie Antoinette was generally hated in France both for her Austrian heritage and her frivolous spending habits.

ers. Some peasants owned their own land, but most rented the land they worked on from the aristocrat who owned it. Peasants often had to work at weaving or labor in the cities by day to supplement their incomes. For the most part, peasants had difficult lives. Urban workers lived in the cities and worked in factories making textiles, glass, paper, or other goods. While they were few in number compared to the rest of the Third Estate, urban workers had a great effect on the Revolution. Their anger at low wages and shortages of bread, their staple food, often spilled over into mob violence during the Revolution. The middle class, or bourgeoisie, could be shopkeepers or wealthy merchants, skilled artisans, government workers, or professionals such as lawyers and doctors—in short, anyone who did not do heavy manual labor for a living.

The Social Hierarchy

In the France of the 1700s there was a wide gap between the wealthy classes and the poor. At the top of the social scale were royalty, wealthy aristocrats, and wealthy and powerful members of the clergy. In the middle was a growing class of merchants and businessmen, many of whom were wealthy and who aspired to become aristocrats. Wealthy members of this middle class were often able to purchase aristocratic offices, titles, and privileges. Many members of the middle class, or bourgeoisie, who had not achieved the rank of nobility resented the privileges and power of the aristocracy who were exempt from taxation and who reserved for themselves the highest positions at court,

A painting symbolizes the meeting of the three classes or estates of the ancien régime. The unequal living conditions between the three estates spawned the revolution.

aristocrat. Noblemen had traditionally lived by the values of loyalty, courage, a refined manner, and service to the king. However, while the aristocrats still claimed the privileges of their estate, many had forgotten their duties and values.

The Third Estate was made up of everyone else—those who were neither members of the clergy nor of the nobility. Three different groups composed the Third Estate. Peasants were mainly farm-

Wealthy couples dance during the period before the French Revolution (left). The lower classes resented the callous attitude most nobles and merchants had toward members of the Third Estate. French peasants led difficult lives. Not only did they have to maintain their farms (below), they often had to work in the city as well to supplement their incomes.

in the church, and in the army. As one historian noted, "Many of the Third Estate wanted equality rather than liberty, [motivated] not so much by an earnest liberalism as by envy and a legitimate [anger]."[5] At the bottom of the social hierarchy were the poor urban workers and peasants who were forced to bear the greatest burden of taxation and who often were barely able to feed themselves and their families. The gap between those at the bottom and those at the top was wide indeed.

Wealthy aristocrats frequently served little purpose in society except as decorations. Often, they were absent from the lands that they owned and whose peasants paid them fees. They spent their time at court, hunting, gambling, playing games or music, or otherwise entertaining themselves in self-serving ways. They wore magnificent clothing and lived in luxurious accommodations.

The palace at Versailles (left) became a symbol of the great inequality between rich and poor. A cartoon (below) poignantly illustrates the great inequality between the estates: A peasant carries the weight of the clergy and nobility upon his back.

Many court nobles were housed at the palace of Versailles, an enormous structure more than half a mile long, located a few miles outside Paris. The palace had been built by Louis XIV at a cost historians estimate at $100 million. Some nobles had their own apartments within the palace, complete with private kitchens and a personal staff of servants. One such apartment had 274 rooms. The grounds were beautifully landscaped, with fountains and beds of brilliant flowers. The royal stables housed nearly two thousand horses, with fifteen hundred grooms to attend them. The royalty and aristocrats also enjoyed enormous privileges in addition to great wealth and luxury. Only aristocrats could gain high positions in the church; only aristocrats could command regiments in the army; only aristocrats could become ambassadors. On the other hand, they were exempt from paying certain taxes: the taille, a tax on the land, and the *corvées royales*, a tax to maintain roads and supply wagons for troop transport. Only commoners and peasants were required to pay these taxes.

The high life of the nobility was a cruel contrast to the terrible poverty of the masses. As Thomas Jefferson observed:

Out of a population of twenty millions of people supposed to be in France . . . there are nineteen millions more wretched, more accursed in every circumstance of human existence, than the most conspicuously wretched individual of the whole United States.[6]

Although not all districts in France were stricken with poverty, many were. An Englishman, Arthur Young, traveled through the countryside shortly before the Revolution, and he observed men and women without shoes or stockings and hungry chil-

The Extravagant Queen

In English Witnesses of the French Revolution, *edited by J. M. Thompson, the dispatches of British diplomat Daniel Hailes criticize Marie Antoinette for her extravagance.*

"The strong propensity of this Princess to every kind of pleasure and expence has been [used to] great advantage by all those who have considered only their own elevation and advancement. Her pretended friends, by administering to her pleasures, [have learned] her secrets, and, having once [learned] of them, they may, in fact, be said to be masters of their own mistress, and to have [made sure to keep] that power, which otherwise the changeableness of her disposition rendered extremely precarious."

To many French citizens, Marie Antoinette's frivolity undermined the monarchy. The unpopular queen was frequently blamed for the corruption of the French court.

dren who were "terribly ragged, if possible worse clad than if with no clothes at all."[7]

Despite their general poverty, peasants were forced to pay harsh taxes. Among the worst and most hated was the *gabelle*, or salt tax. Every commoner over seven years of age was charged a salt tax on seven pounds of salt per year. If there were four people in a family, every year they had to pay a sum equal to nineteen days of labor for salt, whether they needed the salt or not. Peasants who owned land had to pay a taille. Even if crops were poor one year, the amount of tax remained the same. A capitation, or poll tax, was collected on what the land produced, as well as on the income of the people working in the cities.

On top of these taxes, the poor were required to pay ancient feudal dues to the landowner and to observe the landowner's privileges—some foolish, and some painfully costly. For example, the peasants were required to provide food for the manor lord's pigeons. On the other hand, commoners could not keep pigeons, a right reserved for landowners.

Commoners were also required to pay a tithe to the church. In the church, as in the rest of society, the positions of power were held by nobility; however, most of the clergy were poor. The tithe paid by the village peasant often went not to the poor village church but to a rich abbot, an aristocrat, whose monastery had little need of money.

Such taxes were all the more bitter to the common people because the aristocrats were in large part exempt from paying them. The church, rich and powerful as it was, paid no taxes. Instead it contributed a grant to the state every five years. Since the amount of the grant was determined by the church itself, the church was able to exert some control over governmental policies. Even though most clergy were pious and concerned for the people in their care, many aristocratic clergy members were primarily concerned with the efficient running of their large estates and with maintaining their privileges, and they had little concern for the people.

On top of all the heavy taxes commoners had to bear, they were faced with yet another burden—forced military service. Only commoners were required to draw lots for military service, fighting the king's wars wherever he chose to send them. Once in the army, the men were poorly paid and even more poorly fed. They faced serious punishments for the slightest infractions. And as members of the Third Estate, even the brightest were prevented from rising in the ranks—only aristocrats could hold high-ranking positions.

A Seething Anger

Naturally, the common people developed a seething anger and hatred toward the aristocracy, including church leaders. The saying at the time was that it would be a fine day "when the last king might be choked with the entrails of the last priest."[8]

For centuries the ancient feudal society, still in place in eighteenth-century France, had been a just system in which all orders of society fulfilled their responsibilities to one another. The system had served all the people well. But it had degenerated into a system of terrible injustice. As one historian explains:

> In the past, under a feudal system based on landed property, honest and well-meaning Barons . . . had given safety to their dependants, protecting them against invasion [and administering] law; and they were privileged, such privilege being a just [payment] for the fulfilment of their . . . duties. In the age of Louis XIV, when the dangers prevalent during feudal times had almost disappeared, the nobles and high clergy yet retained privilege, and . . . often ignored their . . . duties. Privilege, not founded on equity, had become a national gangrene. While the people were

enduring the moral and physical torment imposed by agents of the Crown and feudal dues, the nobles who were not impoverished attended the Court, uprooted, living and thriving on supplies from folk demoralised by subjection . . . and since the nobles and clergy . . . were exempt from nearly all the more severe taxes, the people supported the ever [growing] financial burdens of France. Privilege had detached itself from service; the duty of safeguarding the people had become an insolent and aggressive right against the people. Masters were absent from their estates, great tracts hitherto cultivated grew rank, justice had devolved into chicanery and corruption.[9]

Clearly, such a system could not survive long. By the 1780s, France's financial crisis was growing daily. The great extravagances of Louis XIV, Louis XV, and finally of Louis XVI and his queen, Marie Antoinette, had nearly emptied the treasury, despite Louis's efforts at reform.

The Philosophes

All the while, new ideas were flourishing, ideas that sought to dispel ignorance, superstition, and the notion of the divine right of kings and the king's right to absolute power. Terms such as "rights of man," "citizen," and "social contract" became part of the political vocabulary of the time. People living in twentieth-century democracies sometimes take for granted that individuals have "certain inalienable rights" that a government cannot take away, such as freedom of speech and freedom of religion. In the eighteenth century, however, these rights were new ideas. Furthermore, people began to consider themselves as "citizens"—individuals with rights as well as responsibilities to their country—not as "subjects" of an absolute monarch who could impose his will upon them. One important philosopher, Jean-Jacques Rousseau, even suggested the notion of a "social contract" between the government and the people. Under the social contract, rulers and ruled shared equal rights as well as specific responsibilities. Citizens agreed to obey the laws and support the government, and in return the government agreed to respect and protect the rights of citizens, to protect their property, and to defend them against foreign invasion, among other

Philosopher Jean-Jacques Rousseau thought the government and the people should enter into a "social contract" where each bore responsibilities to benefit the other.

things. These ideas were the product of the Enlightenment, a period that began in the 1600s and lasted through the 1700s. Scientists such as Isaac Newton and Galileo described reasonable laws for the physical world. In turn, philosophers argued that reason could be applied as well to human nature and affairs. Philosophers believed that just as there were natural laws such as gravity or those that governed the motion of planets, there were natural laws that governed how a society should function. They believed that they could discover those laws through reason. Rousseau's social contract was an example of a society operating according to what he believed were natural laws.

A group of writers and thinkers known as philosophes helped popularize these new ideas of the Enlightenment. One of the most important, François-Marie Arouet de Voltaire, argued against the church and its lack of tolerance for free thought, a freedom considered essential for the discovery of natural laws. Individuals must be allowed to question old superstitions and religious beliefs to arrive at the "truth" of natural laws. The Catholic Church actively discouraged such questioning of old ideas, believing that truth was revealed through the Bible and Church teachings. Voltaire's response to the church was clear: "Crush the infamous thing," he charged. However, Voltaire,

Thomas Jefferson and the Queen

Thomas Jefferson was appointed minister to France in 1785. In his Autobiography, *he lays the entire responsibility for the French Revolution on Marie Antoinette. According to Jefferson, the king would have gone along with the reformers in whatever ways were necessary had it not been for the influence of the queen.*

"But [the king] had a Queen of absolute sway over his weak mind and timid virtue, and of a character the reverse of his in all points. This [woman has] . . . no sound sense, was proud, disdainful of restraint, indignant of all obstacles to her will, eager in the pursuit of pleasure, and firm enough to hold to her desires or perish in their wreck. Her inordinate gambling and dissipations, with those of Count d'Artois and others of her clique, had been [partly responsible for] the exhaustion of the treasury, which called into action the reforming hand of the nation; and her opposition to it, her inflexible perverseness and dauntless spirit, led herself to the guillotine, drew the King on with her, and plunged the world into crimes and calamities which will forever stain the pages of modern history. I have ever believed, that had there been no Queen, there would have been no revolution."

Voltaire's writings greatly influenced the Enlightenment. He raged against the church, believing it had set up unnatural laws and attitudes.

among some liberal-thinking aristocrats such as the Duke d'Aiguillon, the Marquis de Lafayette, Honoré de Mirabeau—all of whom would play important roles in the Revolution—and many others.

As the decade of the 1780s progressed, the stage was set for the Revolution. Even among the aristocrats, contempt for the king and queen was growing. According to Madame de Genlis, governess of the children of the Duke of Orléans:

> You went to pay your respects at Versailles, moaning and groaning all the way: you said over and over that nothing was as boring as Versailles and the Court. . . . Some people in society foresaw troubles and storms, but in general our sense of security was without bounds. . . . We thought of a revolution as something impossible.[10]

Philosopher Montesquieu doubted that the common person was ready for complete freedom and argued that the monarchy must remain in power to govern the populace.

along with another famous philosophe, Montesquieu, doubted that the common people of France were ready for complete freedom. They both proposed a government that gave the king limited power. But another philosophe, Rousseau, disagreed. He believed that human beings are naturally good and that all people should have the right to govern themselves. "Man is born free," he argued, "and everywhere he is in chains." Rousseau believed that a state should be established based on the social contract. What France needed, claimed Rousseau, was a constitution that would establish a limited monarchy, that is, a king who would be answerable to the nation's citizens, not the absolute monarch of old.

These ideas were widely discussed, and they became popular among literate middle-class citizens—doctors, lawyers, government officials, and other professionals. The ideas gained popularity even

Taxing the Poor

In his book The Coming of the French Revolution, *historian Georges Lefebvre explains some of the burdensome taxes imposed on the commoners.*

"The *taille* (the word originally meant the 'cut' taken by the lord from the subject) was the basic tax of the French monarchy before the Revolution. It varied in both form and burdensomeness from province to province, and was never paid by anyone who because of class status, regional privilege or personal influence could obtain exemption, so that not to be *taillable* was one of the most common of privileges, and to be *taillable* was not only a finance expense but a social indignity. In general, the *taille* was paid only by the poor, especially the peasants. . . . Also to be considered as direct taxes, though paid in service rather than in money, were the *corvées royales* consisting in (a) the *transports militaires,* by which civilians lent the use of carts, etc., to assist in troop movements, and above all (b) the *corvée des routes,* by which people within five or ten miles of the through highways or *routes royales* were called upon to supply labor, teams and wagons to keep them in repair, usually being liable for from six to thirty days a year. Only peasants were subject to these *corvées,* though of course it was not mainly the peasants who benefited."

Each group in French society had its own reasons for wanting a change in government. Many aristocrats were jealous of the power of the king and hoped for a limited monarchy in which they could share the power. Many bourgeoisie were jealous of the privileges of the aristocrats. They were also angry about contributing so much to the nation's economy, yet having no say in the government. The peasants and urban workers were outraged by their heavy tax burdens and their often miserable living conditions. And finally, many citizens simply believed that a more just system was long overdue. Yet none of these groups envisioned the sweeping changes the Revolution would bring. Most French citizens did not even realize France was on the brink of revolution. In the words of Alexis de Tocqueville, "Never was any such event so inevitable, yet so completely unforeseen."[11]

2 A Gathering Storm

"I feel the universe is going to fall on me," Louis XVI proclaimed when he ascended the throne in 1774.[12] France, with a population of over twenty million, was the second largest country in Europe (Russia was the largest): a heavy weight indeed for a man of Louis's limitations. All but about one million of the people worked the soil, cultivating barley, oats, and wheat, and raising cows, pigs, horses, and sheep. Only about a half million worked in manufacturing. During the eighteenth century there had been an enormous growth in population, due to better medicine and hygiene, but this increase made it hard to feed all the people.

Louis had inherited enormous problems along with the throne. Louis XV had left a huge debt, corrupt ministers, and a nation clamoring for reform. Louis XVI, who desired nothing more than to be well loved by the people, was ready to make some important reforms. He began by replacing his grandfather's ministers with more honest and efficient men. One of these was the new finance minister, a man named Anne-Robert Turgot who was a friend of the philosophe Voltaire. Liberal thinkers cheered the appointment of Turgot, and Louis was cheered by the approval of the people.

Another important move Louis made was to recall *parlement*, the Paris law court whose members had been exiled by Louis XV. There were thirteen regional *parlements*, or law courts composed of magistrates and lawyers. The Paris *parlement*, whose jurisdiction included about ten million people, was the most powerful. One of its duties was to register royal edicts, especially those having to do with taxation,

As part of an effort to reform the economy, Louis XVI hired Anne-Robert Turgot (below) as finance minister. Turgot's appointment was short-lived, however, as his suggested reforms drew the wrath of the nobility.

The Failure of Reforms

Finance Minister Turgot's efforts at helping the king make reforms seemed doomed to inevitable failure, as historian George Rude explains in The French Revolution.

"Unlike his predecessor, [Louis XVI] had a high sense of personal responsibility. Besides, in his newly appointed Chief Minister, Turgot, he had a man who enjoyed the esteem and affection of both the 'enlightened' and the industrious middle classes. Yet the whole plan collapsed and Turgot was out of office in a couple of years. Why? Turgot's reforms, though welcome to the middle classes, ran counter to the vested interests of the Parlements, the upper clergy and aristocratic factions at Court. . . . And it proved once more, as it was to prove a decade later, that no far-reaching measures of reform were possible, however well intentioned the monarch or honest and able his ministers, so long as the privileged orders were left in possession of their powers through the Parlements and their influence at Court to obstruct the operation. These were the limits beyond which reform could not go—sufficient to whet the appetite of some, to irritate others and satisfy none. Sufficient, too (and this was to prove an important consideration in the future), to draw further hatred on the privileged orders and contempt on the monarchy that appeared to protect them."

before they could become law. Even though in theory the king had absolute power, in the past, *parlement* had exerted some control by refusing to register royal edicts it did not like. Louis's grandfather and great-grandfather had enforced their will by simply exiling *parlement* when it refused to cooperate, thus depriving magistrates of their very well-paid positions.

The appointment of new ministers and the recall of *parlement* seemed to signal a new age. People began to rejoice at the hope of genuine reform. As mathematician and philosopher Jean Le Rond d'Alembert proclaimed, "All the nation shouts in chorus, 'A better day dawns upon us.'"[13]

These hopes did not last long. One of Louis's priorities was to resolve the financial crisis, for which he had counted on Turgot, the new finance minister. Turgot was popular with the enlightened and liberal middle class, but he proved to be an unpopular minister at court. His suggested reforms—to remove restraints on commerce and industry, to impose a tax on nobles and the church, and to redistribute surplus grain—angered nobles, clergy, and farmers alike and finally caused the king to dismiss him.

Turgot was replaced by Jacques Necker, a Swiss banker and self-made millionaire. Necker made enemies of many nobles with his attempts to control the wild spending at court. Necker felt his position was continually undermined by his enemies, and finally demanded that the king grant him more authority. When the king refused, Necker resigned his office. He was replaced by Charles-Alexandre de Calonne. Still, France's financial crisis continued to deepen.

The Assembly of Notables

By 1787, just the interest payments owed by the government on the loans it had taken out amounted to about 50 percent of the money spent by the government. Finance Minster Calonne insisted that the only way out of the difficulty was by equality of taxation—the aristocracy and the church would have to begin to pay their fair share of taxes. However, reforms needed the consent of *parlement*, which could, if it wished, refuse to register these new laws. Knowing that *parlement* would likely resist Calonne's reforms Louis decided on another approach—he called an Assembly of Notables to approve Calonne's plan. The assembly was made up of 144 nobles, both clergy and landed aristocrats, handpicked by the king and Calonne to ensure their cooperation. The king called the meeting at Versailles on February 22, 1787, and explained his purpose: "Gentlemen . . . my plans are far-reaching and important. I intend to relieve the people, increase tax revenue and diminish obstacles to trade."[14]

However, despite the king's pleas, the Assembly of Notables, led by fourteen bishops, opposed most of the plan. The Archbishop of Narbonne declared, "M. de Calonne wishes to bleed France to death. He is merely asking us whether to make the incision on the feet, the arms or the jugular vein."[15] Writers of pamphlets attacked Calonne, spreading the idea that he had spent money foolishly during the previous years and was now passing on the cost to the people. A popular print circulating at the time depicted a monkey speaking to a barnyard of poultry, with the inscription: "My creatures, I have assembled you here to deliberate the sauce in which you will be served."[16]

The Assembly of Notables refused Calonne's plans for taxation, claiming only the Estates General (an advisory body of representatives) could consent to new taxes. People clamored for Calonne's dismissal. Knowing he could not hope to get

Jacques Necker replaced Turgot as finance minister but like Turgot had a difficult time initiating reforms to control the nobility's spending.

his reforms through while Calonne was in office, the king relented and dismissed Calonne.

The Revolt of the Aristocracy

The king, through his new minister, Loménie Brienne, then appealed to the *parlements*, which, as expected, rebelliously refused to consent to reforms. They again insisted that the Estates General be called.

Representatives of the Estates General included members from all three estates: clergy, nobility, and the rest of the people. This institution had not met for 175 years, since 1614, during the reign of Louis XIII. The Estates General was an ancient institution, established before the development of the absolute monarchy. In its original form, the institution gave advice to the king and voted on establishing taxes. As the power of the monarchy grew, the kings of France had increasingly less use for the Estates General and called it only in times of financial crisis, to support the king's demands for taxation. Louis XVI knew that by calling the Estates General, he would be admitting that his power was less than absolute; furthermore, he knew that his enemies among the nobility could use the Estates General to limit his power and gain more power for themselves. Thus, Louis was not willing to give in to the demands of the *parlements* by calling the Estates General. Instead, he decided to use force. In May of 1788, he dismissed all the *parlements* and had the leading members of the Paris *parlement* arrested. Violent protests erupted throughout the country. The aristocracy enlisted the support of lawyers, judges, government officials, and other members of the Third Estate in opposing the absolute power of the king.

The alliance between the aristocracy and the Third Estate finally defeated the king. Brienne was forced to resign, and the king recalled Necker, abolished the reform plans, and restored *parlement*. More importantly, he agreed that the Estates General should meet in May 1789.

The aristocracy felt it had achieved its aims and that the king's power was checked. However, the aristocracy could

To help get financial reforms passed, the king appointed the Assembly of Notables in 1787. Even though the hand-picked members were supposed to agree to tax reform, they balked and refused to pass the much needed laws.

Holding On to Power

Even though the aristocracy had enlisted the aid of the Third Estate in limiting the king's power, the nobility had no intention of sharing their new power with the people. In his book The French Revolution 1787-1799, *noted French historian Albert Soboul explains the aristocracy's motivations.*

"The aristocracy had not hesitated to use violent methods against royal government in defence of their privileges. The [aristocracy and the clergy] had allied in refusing to obey the King and had called to their aid the middle classes who were in this act of defiance serving their apprenticeship in revolution-making. But if the aristocracy were demanding a constitutional regime and the guarantee of their basic liberties, if they were claiming the right to vote taxes for the Estates General and the return of local administration to elective provincial estates, it was no less their intention to maintain within these various bodies their own political and social [power]. . . . The nobility were unanimous in demanding the retention of feudal and especially of honorific rights. The aristocracy did indeed start the struggle against absolute monarchy and they involved the Third Estate in that campaign, but they did so with the clear intention of establishing on the ruins of absolutism their own political power and of ensuring that their social privileges were not endangered."

---

not know that it had unleashed forces that would change French society forever. As historian Albert Soboul explains:

> At the end of September 1788 the aristocracy was victorious. But if the aristocratic revolt had checked the activities of the King, it had at the same time shaken the monarchy sufficiently to open the way for that revolution for which economic and social changes were preparing the Third Estate. The Third now took the floor in its turn and the real Revolution began.[17]

The treasury was out of money, and the people were demanding an end to the absolute power of the king. As if these were not problems enough for Louis to face, France was in the midst of an economic depression. By 1788, unemployment was a serious problem. There was a poor harvest in 1788 that caused the price of bread to rise dramatically. Since bread was a staple of the French diet—most working people ate between three and four pounds of bread in a day—many faced starvation. People began rioting. By the spring of 1789, people were hungry, angry, and beginning to claim that the aristocracy was hoarding grain to gain their own political ends. It was in this atmosphere that the Estates General was to meet.

Chapter

3 The Revolution Begins

The Hall of Mirrors was one of the most magnificent salons of the grand palace at Versailles. It was decorated with gilded sculpture, rich marble, and fourteen silver and crystal chandeliers. At night, light from chandeliers was reflected in over three hundred Venetian mirrors, creating a breathtaking sight.

On May 2, 1789, the king received the deputies of the Estates General in this impressive room. First came the clergy, according to custom, and then the nobility. Finally, after a wait of three hours, the deputies of the Third Estate were received, not in the magnificent Hall of Mirrors, but in another apartment, in which they were quickly ushered in processional file past the king. Deputies of the Third Estate were disheartened at their reception. The king had made it clear that he wished to keep the traditional distinctions among the estates.

What Is the Third Estate?

Louis's reception of the Third Estate was an indication that the common people would have to continue to fight for their interests. In September 1788, the Paris *parlement* had announced that the Estates

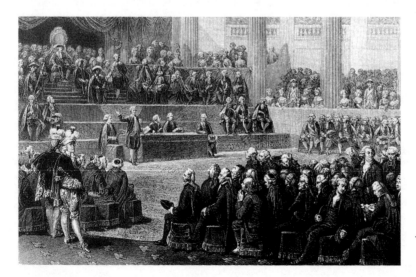

The meeting of the Estates General in 1789. The meeting was protested by members of the Third Estate, who were at first excluded from meeting in the same room as members of the clergy and nobility.

30 ■ THE FRENCH REVOLUTION

General would be called; it also declared that the Estates should be composed as it had been in 1614. The three orders—clergy, nobility, and Third Estate—would have an equal number of deputies, even though the number of people in France belonging to the Third Estate far outnumbered the members in the other two orders. According to the custom, each order would take a vote of its members separately, and then the three orders would meet to cast their three separate votes. This meant that nobility and clergy could combine their votes to defend their interests against the Third Estate.

When members of the Third Estate realized they would have little voice in the Estates General because of the system of voting, they quickly turned against the Paris *parlement* and the privileged classes. According to one historian:

> In the autumn and winter of 1788, the struggle between the monarchy and the aristocracy was transformed into a social and political conflict between the privileged and unprivileged classes. As the issues broadened, the solidarity of the privileged orders weakened. A split appeared even in the ranks of the parlement of Paris between conservative magistrates and those with liberal inclinations.[18]

A contemporary journalist, Jacques Mallet du Pan, observed that the political issues had changed radically. The difficulties were no longer constitutional issues between the king and the privileged estates, but "a war between the Third Estate and the other two orders."[19]

Everywhere there was talk of politics. Political pamphlets were published at an incredible rate and passed feverishly from

Abbé Emmanuel-Joseph Sièyes had a deep compassion for the downtrodden, but was a poor public speaker and had a difficult time conveying his ideas publicly until he turned to writing.

hand to hand. One of the most popular pamphleteers was the Abbé Emmanuel-Joseph Sièyes. As a young man he had wanted to join the army, but at the insistence of his parents he became a clergyman. A well-educated man, Sièyes rose in the church hierarchy. But since he was not a member of the aristocracy, he had no hope of becoming a bishop, a fact that caused him to develop hostility toward the aristocracy. Sièyes was a thin, small, austere man, uncomfortable in society but deeply concerned with the condition of the poor. He had a weak voice and, as one listener observed, an "ungraceful and ineloquent"

What Is the Third Estate?

What Is the Third Estate? by Abbé Sieyès had an enormous influence on the Revolution, as described by J. M. Thompson in Leaders of the French Revolution.

"In 1788 Necker announced that the States-General would meet early in the next year and invited public discussion of the situation. Sièyes, who had reached his fortieth year without breaking his philosophic silence, was moved to write, and found that he had the gift of lucid expression. His first two pamphlets did not catch popular attention, but the third, issued in January, 1789, with the clever title, [*What Is the Third Estate?*], at once made history. . . . In the famous debate of June 15-16, which decided that there should be a revolution, most of the talking was done by Mirabeau, but most of the ideas came from Sièyes' pamphlet. It was in the course of these sessions that Arthur Young heard Sièyes speak 'ungracefully and ineloquently, but logically.' . . . From this moment, though his voice was weak, and his manner cold, he was always attended to."

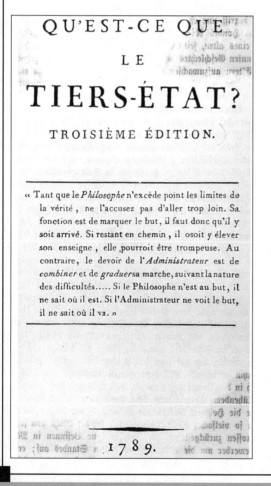

The title page of Sièyes pamphlet. In it, he argued that the Third Estate was being denied its rightful place in government decision making.

manner as an orator. But Sièyes soon found a way to influence reform—persuasive writing. His pamphlet *What Is the Third Estate?* was one of the most influential of the time. He answered the question he asked in the pamphlet's title: "Everything. What has it been up till now in the political order? Nothing. What does it desire to be? Something."[20] In his pamphlet, Sièyes argued that the Third Estate should have the same number of representatives as the other two orders combined. He also argued that the votes of the Estates General should be by head, that is, the Estates General should vote as a single body—one vote per representative regardless of estate or order.

A New Method of Voting

The manner of voting Sièyes proposed would make a significant difference in a vote's outcome. Under the old method of voting, each estate met separately to vote on an issue, such as a new tax. Each estate would either pass or fail to pass the tax. The three estates would then meet, and each estate would cast its one vote according to whether the issue had passed or failed in its separate session. This vote "by order" meant that the two privileged estates or orders, clergy and nobility, could vote to impose a new tax on Third Estate members. Since the Third Estate had only one vote to cast, the other two orders could always combine their two votes, thus assuring that they maintained their privileges. Sièyes wanted the Third Estate to have twice as many representatives and have the Estates General vote as a single body, taking the vote "by head." This meant that the vote would be taken at a joint meeting of the Estates General, with each individual

casting his vote for or against the issue. If the Third Estate had the same number of representatives as the other two orders combined, this vote "by head" meant that the Third Estate would have a total number of votes equal to that of the other two orders. The clergy and nobility would thus lose their advantage if votes were taken "by head," giving the Third Estate a real voice in the Estates General.

In December of 1788, the king gave in to pressure and announced that the Third Estate should have an equal number of representatives as the other two orders combined. However, there was no promise of how the voting would take place—by order or by head.

Across the country the process of electing deputies to the Estates General began. In towns and cities, electoral assemblies met to choose their deputies and at the same time to draw up lists of grievances, called *cahiers de doléances*. The cahiers were surprisingly similar. All three orders denounced absolutism and called for a constitution limiting the monarch's power and establishing a national assembly to vote on taxes and make laws. All three orders agreed that the tax system needed reform and that freedom of the press and personal liberty should be guaranteed. However, the clergy generally rejected the notion of freedom of religious conscience—they were determined to maintain control over the people's religious beliefs and practices. Further, they said nothing about the issue of the privileges, such as freedom from certain taxes, that the clergy and nobility enjoyed.

The nobility defended the idea of voting by order, which they believed was a way to protect their privileges; they rejected the idea of equal rights and of equality in all forms of employment. The nobility wanted to retain their exclusive right to hold high rank in the army, to serve in high positions in the church and in the government, and to other privileged employment that was denied to members of the Third Estate.

The Third Estate was nearly unanimous in its claim for equality in every area, for the abolition of tithes to the church, and for the suppression of feudal dues.

Not all members within each order were necessarily in agreement. Within the clergy, parish priests were more inclined to side with the poor than with the aristocratic bishops. There were disputes among the aristocracy—some petty feuding and some genuine disagreement between provincial nobles and the nobles at court. Furthermore, a number of nobles were sympathetic to the demands of the Third Estate.

Finally, during the first week of May 1789, the deputies were ready to assemble at Versailles for the meeting of the Estates General, the first in 175 years. After they were received by the king on Saturday, May 2, 1789, they prepared for their first meeting.

The Estates General Meets

Monday, May 4, the deputies of the three orders marched in solemn procession through Versailles to attend a special mass at the Church of St. Louis. Each order marched separately, and the members were dressed by ancient custom according to their order. First were deputies of the Third Estate dressed in the official black suits with cambric ruffs and wearing hats called tricornes. Following them came nobles, splendidly dressed in black satin suits with lace ruffs, silver waistcoats and trimmings, plumed hats, and swords at their sides. Next came clergy, first the parish priests dressed in plain black robes followed by members of the church hierarchy dressed in purple and scarlet episcopal robes. Finally, the king and queen proceeded to the church. According to one observer, "The King is repeat-

Before the Estates General met, they held a magnificent procession in which each member was dressed in the traditional costume of his order.

edly saluted as he passes along with the *Vive le Roi!* [long live the king!] but the Queen receives not a single acclamation. She looks, however, with contempt on the scene in which she acts a part."[21]

The procession was a magnificent spectacle designed to impress the populace and inspire patriotic loyalty to France and to the king. Very few people recognized the real significance of the event. Madame de Staël, daughter of Finance Minister Jacques Necker, watched the procession from her window and recorded this conversation:

> I was placed at a window near Madame de Montmorin, the wife of the minister of foreign affairs, and I abandoned myself, I must admit to the keenest hope, seeing for the first time in France the representatives of the nation. Mme de Montmorin, whose mind was in no way distinguished, said with a decisive tone, which made an impression upon me: "You are wrong to rejoice. The results will be disastrous both for France and for us."[22]

The next day, the Estates General convened in a hall redecorated for the occasion. Dressed in a cloth-of-gold suit with the huge Regent diamond adorning his hat, the king entered the hall to shouts of "*Vive le Roi!*" He was followed by the queen, who wore a white dress decorated with silver and a heron plume in her hair. Taking his seat on the velvet-covered throne, Louis addressed the assembly:

> Gentlemen, the day I have been eagerly waiting for has arrived, and I find myself surrounded by the representatives of the nation which it is my glory to command. . . . A general rest-

At the first meeting of the Estates General, Jacques Necker gave a long speech detailing France's financial condition.

lessness and an exaggerated desire for change have captured men's minds and would end by leading public opinion completely astray were they not to be given proper direction by your wisdom and moderation.[23]

Thus Louis made his position clear. He would accept some changes, yes, but nothing too dramatic.

The final speaker of the day was Jacques Necker, who gave a long speech lasting over three hours about France's financial condition. Occasionally he had an assistant read parts of the speech when his voice needed a rest. However, despite the speech's length, Necker mentioned nothing of political matters or how the votes would be taken, by order or by head. Finally the meeting ended, with the deputies of the Third Estate disappointed.

The Flurry of Pamphlets

The meeting of the Estates General aroused intense interest, and political pamphlets were being published at an astonishing rate. J. M. Thompson, editor of English Witnesses of the French Revolution, *quotes the observations of Arthur Young, an English traveler in France during that period.*

"The business going forward at present in pamphlet shops of Paris is incredible. I went to the Palais Royal to see what new things were published, and to procure a catalogue of all. Every hour produces something new. Thirteen came out today, sixteen yesterday, and ninety-two last week. . . . This spirit of reading political tracts, they say, spreads into the provinces so that all the presses of France are equally employed. Nineteen-twentieths of these productions are in favour of liberty, and commonly violent against the clergy and nobility. . . . But the coffeehouses in the Palais Royal present yet more singular and astonishing spectacles; they are not only crowded within, but other expectant crowds are at the doors and windows, listening . . . to certain orators, who from chairs or tables harangue each his little audience: the eagerness with which they are heard, and the thunder of applause they receive for every sentiment of more than common hardiness or violence against the present government, cannot easily be imagined."

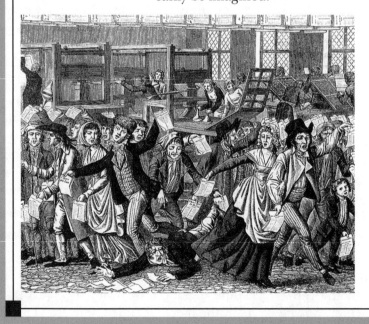

As the Estates General met, the populace became fascinated with the ongoing discussions, rushing out to buy revolutionary handbills and newspapers that commented on the meetings.

According to custom, following the opening meeting, each of the three orders were to meet separately to take up their business. That evening, deputies of the Third Estate met among themselves to discuss what steps should be taken to ensure that their voices would be heard. One common theme arose: the deputies would refuse to meet independently of the other two orders—they would somehow have to force a vote by head.

The next day the clergy and nobility each met in separate halls set aside for them. However, the Third Estate refused to meet separately and remained in the large hall, insisting that all three orders meet together. The hall was open to the public, and people crowded around the deputies, cheering and encouraging them, offering advice.

Support from the Clergy

In the meantime, both nobility and clergy had voted against the idea of combining the three orders and allowing each representative an individual vote. However, many poor parish priests were in sympathy with the Third Estate. As one priest bitterly reminded the assembly, "The village priests may not have the talents of Academicians but they have at least the sound common sense of villagers!"[24] Even though the poor priests were not able to influence their order to vote in favor of combining the three orders, their support of the Third Estate would soon become an important factor. Despite the votes by the other two orders, the Third Estate remained adamant in its insistence on combined voting, which it considered crucial if

any real reforms were to take place. According to historian Albert Soboul:

> The question was of such overwhelming importance that there could be no bargaining. . . . There were only two possibilities: either nobility—for it was the nobility that was playing the leading role among the two privileged orders— gave way, in which case privileges would be ended and a new era would begin; or else the Third would have to admit defeat, which would mean the maintenance of the Ancien Regime.[25]

The standoff continued, amid much confusion. Supposedly, the Estates General was in session, but no business was taking place. Finally, in early June, pamphleteer Abbé Sièyes, who had been elected a deputy to the Third Estate from the Paris district, suggested that the Third Estate declare itself the true representative body of France and invite the other two orders to join. Sièyes's suggestion was agreed upon. After inviting deputies of other estates to join them, the deputies of the Third Estate announced that on June 12 they would begin a roll call of all members of the Estates General, whether the members of the other orders were present or not. They would then begin the business of the meeting. That threat broke the stalemate. Nineteen members of the clergy—the village priests who had earlier argued in favor of combining the three orders—joined the deputies of the Third Estate.

On June 15, Abbé Sièyes proposed that the deputies begin working on the constitution. Sièyes further suggested abandoning the title "Estates General," since the name had lost its meaning, and replacing it with another name. Deputies began a lively debate about new names for their assembly. Sièyes had suggested "Assembly of Representatives Recognized and Verified by the French Nation." Another deputy recommended "The Legitimate Assembly of the Representatives of the Major Part of the Nation, Acting in the Absence of the Minor Part." Finally, someone suggested the name "National Assembly," and on June 17, the Third Estate voted to accept that name as their new designation.

On June 19, the clergy voted that the Estates General should meet as a general assembly of all three orders. The nobility were more stiff-necked, however. On that same day, June 19, they addressed a letter to the king:

> If the rights which we are defending were our rights and ours alone, if they concerned no one but the order of the nobility, then we should be showing less enthusiasm in claiming them and less determination in defending them. But it is not merely our own interests that we are protecting, Sire, it is yours and those of the State, and, in the last analysis, those of the French people.[26]

The king was encouraged by the nobility's stand, and he and his council decided that day to oppose the actions of the Third Estate. Louis ordered that the great hall where the Third Estate held its meetings be closed.

The Tennis Court Oath

"I am a mad dog from whose bites despotism and privilege will die"—thus Honoré-Gabriel Riqueti de Mirabeau, one of the Revolution's great leaders, characterized

himself.[27] Mirabeau was a powerful, magnetic speaker, and though he was a nobleman, he was popular with the common people, who elected him as a deputy from the Third Estate. Despite his reputation for vanity, immorality, rudeness, and arrogance, he quickly became a leader among

Revolutionary Gabriel Riqueti de Mirabeau was a forceful speaker for government reform and constitutional monarchy. Largely due to his stubborn efforts, the Third Estate was allowed to meet jointly with members of the clergy and nobility.

Paris on the Threshold of Revolution

There was a lively, happy atmosphere in the Paris of 1789. Parisians seemed to feel they were on the threshold of great events. In Three Weeks in Paris During the Revolution, *the German bookseller and writer Campe describes his impressions during his visit.*

"Among the thousands of people who cross the Pont-Neuf [bridge], the twenty or thirty thousand that swarm in the Tuileries, or on the boulevards, one hardly ever sees a single person walking slowly, [listlessly], hardly one whose hands and facial features are not in perpetual movement, and if two or more people are walking together, the thread of their [conversation] is never broken. . . . This gives the Parisian crowd a distinction that can be found nowhere else: it is more vivacious, more noisy than any other crowd in the world. Everybody is talking, singing, shouting or whistling, instead of proceeding in silence, as is the custom in our parts. And the multitude of street-vendors and small merchants trying to make their voices heard above the tumult of the streets only serves to make the general uproar all the greater and more deafening."

the deputies. Mirabeau had a striking appearance, characterized by many as ugly. He was massive in size, with a large head set on a thick neck, and bulging, intense eyes. His hair, a thick mass of powdered curls, swept back from his face like a mane. His face was heavily scarred with pockmarks from a childhood bout with smallpox. Mirabeau had enormous energy and some observers likened him to a force of nature. Despite his unpleasant appearance, Mirabeau projected a powerful magnetism that both attracted women and lent power to his speech.

Mirabeau passionately believed that the government must be reformed. He was committed to justice and equality and firmly believed that a constitutional monarchy was the best way to achieve those ends and maintain order in France. And so, on the morning of June 20, when deputies arrived to find that their meeting hall doors were locked, Mirabeau was not going to give up. The meeting was moved to an empty building nearby, one of the royal tennis courts. A young deputy named Jean-Joseph Mounier declared that all deputies should swear never to disband until they had drafted a constitution. All deputies, with the exception of one, took the famous Tennis Court Oath.

The king called a special session of the Estates General three days later and insisted that the three orders meet separately. As he ended the speech, Louis ordered the Estates General to disperse and return the next day to their own separate meeting places. He then promptly left

Members of the Third Estate swear to remain united until they are allowed to draft a new constitution. Because they met in a building that housed the royal tennis courts, the oath was called the Tennis Court Oath.

the hall. The nobles and some clergy obeyed his order, but the new National Assembly refused to leave. Mirabeau reminded the deputies of their oath. When they were again ordered to leave by the master of ceremonies, Mirabeau replied in his bold, resounding voice, "Go tell your master that we are here by the will of the people and that we shall not stir from our seats unless forced to do so by bayonets." When the king was told that the deputies were still in the hall, he responded "Well, damn it, let them stay."[28]

In a few days, the National Assembly was joined by more clergy and by some members of the nobility. Finally, on June 27, the king gave his approval for the joint meeting of the Estates General. The king was defeated. The deputies of the Third Estate had won their point—the National Assembly would represent all the people. The Revolution had begun.

Chapter

4 Bastille and the Summer of Violence

Paris in 1789 was a city of extremes: a few broad avenues such as the Champs Élysées that were wide enough for a royal procession of thousands contrasted with the poor districts' narrow, winding, muddy streets, not wide enough for two carts to pass each other. Magnificent buildings such as the palace at the Tuileries with its adjoining gardens and the grand Cathedral of Notre Dame stood in contrast to the small, miserable wooden buildings housing poor workers. The city was divided into districts, or sections, each having its own atmosphere.

There were districts occupied by nobility and rich bourgeoisie, where streets were wide and houses were grand. In the working class districts, workers in the same trade congregated: There was a district where stonemasons lived, a district where furniture builders lived, and so on. The sections in Paris were like small towns; the inhabitants were occupied in the same trade, shopped at the local market, spent time at the local tavern, usually married someone from their section, and lived their entire lives within a section, rarely leaving it.

Paris was noted both for its beautiful architecture, such as the Cathedral of Notre Dame, pictured here, and its miserable wooden hovels, which housed the poor.

For the most part there was little contact between the wealthy and noble Parisians and the Parisian workers. An exception was Paris's most important—and notorious—meeting place, the Palais Royal. Built by the Duke of Orléans, cousin and political enemy of the king, the Palais Royal was an arcade that included cafés, shops, theaters, and restaurants. A visitor to the Palais Royal might see a strolling guitarist playing bawdy songs, attend a theater featuring three-foot-tall marionettes; the visitor could shop at a wig maker's or a lace maker's, play checkers or chess in outdoor cafés, buy the latest political pamphlet at a bookstore, and at precisely noon see a miniature cannon fire when struck by the sun's rays. As one popular writer of the time described it, "This enchanted place is a small luxurious city enclosed in a large one."[29] It was a place where nobility and wealthy bourgeoisie mixed with pickpockets and prostitutes, and where political agitators harangued listeners about the evils of the government wherever they could gather an audience. It was here that the popular Revolution began.

The Dismissal of Necker

In June of 1789, the Third Estate had won their point—there was now a National Assembly—but the people were still hungry. The price of bread continued to rise, and the poor from the countryside arrived in Paris daily to search for work. By July of 1789, nearly half of the workers in Paris were unemployed, and the price of a loaf of bread was half a day's wage for some workers.

The Palais Royal

Politics and the ideas of the philosophes were ardently discussed at the fashionable Palais Royal. In Daily Life in the French Revolution, *author Jean Robiquet quotes a letter of a provincial visitor to the Palais Royal, the Marquis de Ferrières, who describes the place.*

"You simply cannot imagine all the different kinds of people who gather there. It is a truly astonishing spectacle. I saw the circus; I visited five or six cafés, and no Molière comedy could have done justice to the variety of scenes I witnessed. Here a man is drafting a reform of the Constitution; another is reading his pamphlet aloud; at another table, someone is taking the ministers to task; everybody is talking; each person has his own little audience that listens very attentively to him. I spent almost ten hours there. The paths are swarming with girls and young men. The bookshops are packed with people browsing through books and pamphlets and not buying anything. In the cafés, one is half-suffocated by the press of people."

Meanwhile, the king, realizing that he was losing control of his government to the National Assembly, began to call in troops from the country's borders to the outskirts of Paris. The National Assembly protested. In a speech on July 8, Mirabeau angrily declared:

> A large number of troops already surround us. More are arriving each day. Artillery are being brought up. . . . These preparations for war are obvious to anyone and fill every heart with indignation.[30]

Tensions escalated on July 12. Many of the king's ministers wanted the king to dismiss Finance Minister Jacques Necker, who had encouraged the king to give in to the Third Estate's demands. Finally, Louis dismissed Necker, but when the news reached Paris, people were enraged. The people saw Necker as their ally and their hero. Without him, the people feared that the country would face bankruptcy and that there would be less work, and less bread as well. The workers already suspected that aristocrats had been withholding grain in order to destroy the Third Estate, and now their fears seemed confirmed. It was, after all, the aristocrats who had forced Necker's resignation.

Meanwhile, the National Assembly realized it was in great danger. The deputies knew that the king could send troops to disband their assembly at any time, and they had no power to stop him.

Camille Desmoulins and the Green Cockade

Camille Desmoulins was a pale, weak young man with dark, restless eyes and un-

Camille Desmoulins seemed an unlikely candidate to rouse the revolutionaries. Having failed at his law studies, he lived a life of poverty as a copier.

kempt, long curly hair. He was passionate and brilliant, but sullen and sometimes bitter. He had studied law, but was not successful in that field, and he spent much of his time in Paris in poverty, making a scant income copying legal documents and writing radical pamphlets. Desmoulins joined one of the new political clubs that were flourishing throughout Paris, a club that would become known as the Jacobins. There Desmoulins became a friend of Mirabeau. Desmoulins—passionate, vain, and burning with ambition—was determined to make his mark in these tumultuous times.

On July 12, as news reached Paris of Necker's dismissal, Desmoulins felt his time had come. He rushed to the Palais Royal, where huge crowds had collected. Leaping on a café table, he shouted to the crowd:

Citizens, you know that the nation asked for Necker to stay . . . and now he's been driven out! . . . After this, they will stop at nothing. Tonight they are plotting . . . a massacre of patriots.[31]

Desmoulins had rehearsed this moment, and he had prepared himself well. With all the drama he could muster, he cried, "To arms, to arms!" Placing a green ribbon on his hat, he cried, "Let us all take a green cockade, the color of hope." And in a bit of stage acting, he pulled a pistol from his coat, shouting, "Yes, yes, it is I who call my brothers to freedom: I would die rather than submit to servitude."[32] The people went wild. Desmoulins was an instant hero whom they carried off with great shouting and cheering. People tore

Desmoulins rouses the people to take up arms against those in power. The crowds quickly became an unmanageable mob.

leaves off trees or seized anything they could find that was green to place as cockades in their hats.

Soon angry mobs roamed the city, breaking into shops to loot guns, swords, knives—any weapons they could find. They threatened the homes of wealthy citizens and pillaged bakers' shops. The crowd was becoming dangerously unmanageable.

In response to the crisis, the Paris Electors, the group who had elected the Parisian deputies to the Estates General, met at first light on July 13 at the Hôtel de Ville, where they decided to organize a militia composed of respectable citizens. The militia was organized to defend the interests of property owners, not only against royal troops but against the rioting mobs. Since no uniform could be issued on such short notice, it was decided that the citizen militia should wear the colors of Paris—red and blue—in their hats.

"To the Bastille!"

On Tuesday morning, July 14, heavy clouds hung over the city, threatening rain. During the previous night, rioting had continued as rumors flew through the city of thousands of the king's soldiers massing to attack. Some of the royal troops in Paris had given their support to the citizens. Royal authority in the city was quickly breaking down.

As dawn broke, thousands of people gathered on the royal parade grounds in front of the Hôtel Invalides, the army's arsenal where guns were stored, demanding arms. Soon the rioters had carried off about thirty thousand muskets and several

French citizens storm the courtyard of the Hôtel Invalides to obtain the weapons stored there. When they found little ammunition, they quickly moved on to the Bastille (below) where it was stored.

cannons, but they found very little gunpowder and few bullets. Fearing the crowds, the governor had sent the ammunition to the fortified prison of the Bastille for safekeeping. When the crowd learned where the ammunition was stored, the cry went up: "To the Bastille! To the Bastille!"

The Bastille had been built as a fortress in the fourteenth century. It was a large building with walls five feet thick that linked eight round towers; its entrance was protected with a drawbridge to its outer court and with a second drawbridge to the inner court. No longer needed as a fortress, it was used to hold political prisoners. Although the conditions of the prison were relatively humane for the times, the Bastille was a symbol of the oppression of the Bourbon kings.

In command of the Bastille was Bernard de Launay, a man described by one of his soldiers as being "without much knowledge of military affairs, without experience and without much courage."[33] Launay commanded a garrison of thirty-

two Swiss soldiers and eighty-two elderly French soldiers, or *invalides*.

As the crowd surrounded the Bastille's entrance, the Paris Electors, who had set up a permanent committee to oversee the crisis, asked Launay to remove the cannon from the walls, since it was a threat to the people, and not to resist if attacked. Launay agreed to remove the cannon, but insisted he would defend the Bastille to the death.

Shortly after noon, the crowd attacked, destroying the first drawbridge. As the news spread throughout the city, hundreds of people thronged to the site, including members of the French Guard. Cannons were brought in and aimed at the second drawbridge. The Bastille defenders began firing into the crowd. Realizing his hopeless situation, Launay finally sent a note to the French Guard, agreeing to surrender to them if he were treated with the dignity of a military prisoner. The last drawbridge was lowered and the mob poured into the fortress, killing those few soldiers who were still armed and releasing the Bastille's seven prisoners. In all, about a hundred citizens were killed in the attack.

Launay was taken prisoner. He was marched off through the crowd toward the Hôtel de Ville. However, his guards could not protect him from the mob's fury. They murdered Launay, cut off his head, and mounted it on a pike. Along with a pike bearing the head of another unfortunate victim, the mob carried Launay's severed head to the Palais Royal.

The Bastille had fallen, and the citizens of Paris were ecstatic. But not everyone received the news with joy. When Louis was awakened early on the morning of the 15th and told of the fall of the Bastille, he supposedly asked, "Is this a rebellion?" The official who had awakened him replied, "No sire, it is a revolution." The deputies at the National Assembly in

To Arms!

Workers throughout Paris were feverishly taking up arms to assault the Bastille. In The Days of the French Revolution, *author Christopher Hibbert quotes a Swiss watchmaker named Jean Baptiste Humbert, who describes his experience on July 14.*

"I was accosted by a citizen who told me they were now issuing shot at the Hôtel de Ville. So I hurried there and was given a few pellets of buckshot. I then immediately set out for the Bastille, loading my gun as I went. I was joined by a group of people who were also on their way to the Bastille. We found four foot-soldiers of the Watch, armed with guns and I urged them to come along with us. They replied they had neither powder nor shot. So we clubbed together to give each of them enough for two shots. Thus armed they were pleased to join us. As we were passing in front of the Hôtel de la Régie we saw that two cases of bullets had just been broken up and their contents were being freely handed out. I filled one of my coat pockets with them to give to anyone who was short. . . . [Then], passing through the courtyard of the Arsenal, we arrived at the Bastille."

Unruly crowds storm the Bastille, releasing prisoners (below) and arresting Bernard de Launay (left), commander of the Bastille. In spite of promises to the contrary, the crowds quickly executed de Launay.

Paris received the news with anxiety. What would the king do now? According to Victorine de Chastenay, daughter of a liberal aristocratic deputy to the assembly:

> Versailles was in a stupor and the deputies in dread. . . . Blood had been spilled by the people . . . and the King, blessed by the people scarcely three months earlier, was now at war with that same people.[34]

However, in Paris, the Paris Electors took full advantage of the situation by seizing the city's government. The Permanent Committee became the Paris Commune, claiming the Hôtel de Ville as city hall and electing as mayor Jean Sylvain Bailly, a Paris deputy to the National Assembly. The Marquis de Lafayette who had fought in the American Revolution, was appointed as the commander of the Paris militia, which became known as the National Guard.

The king decided on a tactical retreat. On the 16th, two days after the fall of the Bastille, Louis recalled Jacques Necker. Louis further agreed to appear in Paris on the 17th. The night before, the king's brother and other nobles, horrified by the crumbling monarchy, left for the Netherlands. Before Louis left for Paris the morning of the 17th, he wrote his last will, believing that he would never return to Versailles. Yet his reception in Paris was surprisingly warm. Bailly, the new mayor, greeted him and handed him a tricolor cockade, the emblem of the Revolution. (White, the color of the Bourbons, had been added to the original red and blue denoting Paris.) Louis placed the cockade

The Return of Necker

In Blood Sisters, *author Marilyn Yalom quotes the daughter of Jacques Necker, the noted writer Madame de Staël, who describes Necker's triumphant return to Paris after the fall of the Bastille.*

"The entire population of Paris turned out en masse in the streets. One saw women and men at their windows and on the roofs crying out: Long live Monsieur Necker. When he arrived near the City Hall, the cheers redoubled. The square was filled with a multitude of people animated by the same emotion. They all followed the steps of one man, and that man was my father. . . . Monsieur Necker then advanced to the balcony, and when he proclaimed in a loud voice the holy words of peace between Frenchmen of all parties, the whole multitude responded enthusiastically. I saw nothing more at that moment, because I fainted from sheer joy."

in his hat and entered the hall. Bailly described his reception:

> Applause and shouts of *Vive le Roi!* welcomed him on every side. All eyes, filled with tears, were turned towards him. The people held out their hands to him. And when he was placed on the throne which had been prepared for him, a voice from the back of the assembly uttered the heartfelt cry: "Our King! Our father!" At this applause, the excitement, the shouts of *Vive le Roi!* redoubled.[35]

Later, Louis walked out on the balcony to greet the crowd. When they saw the cockade in his hat they responded with great shouts of joy, prepared to give him their wholehearted approval. Louis had accepted the Revolution. The evil advisers had been dismissed, and the hated court aristocrats had left the country. It seemed that this relatively bloodless revolution was complete.

Peasants, Sansculotte, and the Popular Revolt

Not everyone was satisfied, however. Throughout the spring and summer of 1789, peasants had waited impatiently for results from their deputies to the Third Estate in Versailles. The bourgeoisie had achieved some of their own aims, and the workers in Paris had achieved a glorious victory in storming the Bastille. But the peasants were still suffering under feudal laws. In addition, many of them were hungry. Unemployment and food shortages were severe, and people wandered the roads begging for a living. People were convinced there was an aristocratic plot aimed at suppressing all change. Popular discontent and anxiety were spreading. With the fall of the Bastille, common people took matters into their own hands. Peasants rioted, destroying fences and walls on manor lands, slaughtering game in the manorial forests, killing the landowners' pigeons and raiding their fishponds, and sometimes invading châteaus and assaulting the manor lord. Bands of rioters forced the manor lords to turn over old documents that in the distant past had given lords the right to collect rents and exact levies on local peasants. The documents were burned in huge bonfires in the village squares.

Workers in towns and cities began rioting as well, taking their cue from their counterparts in Paris. The working class became known as sansculotte, meaning "without knee breeches" (a reference to the fashionable knee breeches worn by aristocrats). They became an important force in the Revolution. Rioting workers were mainly concerned with the high price of bread, and their targets were often bakers, millers, or grain dealers.

Side by side with the sporadic violence of the popular revolt, a municipal revolution was taking place. In towns and cities throughout France, people were making changes in their local governments. The municipal revolution was carried out primarily by bourgeois citizens, who were often as fearful of the peasants as were the aristocratic landowners. In nearly all provinces a local bourgeois militia was formed, patterned after the National Guard in Paris, to keep order in the area. The common theme of the municipal revolution throughout France was the overthrow of centralized authority and the

Male and female members of the sansculotte sport their distinctive outfits. The sansculotte became an important part of the revolution.

diminishment of royal power. Local government flourished throughout the country, which had long suffered under royal absolutism.

The Great Fear

The peasant rioting, the disturbances throughout the country, and the readiness to believe even the most far-fetched rumors led to the period of events known as the Great Fear.

Like wildfire, the Great Fear suddenly broke out, sweeping uncontrollably across the countryside. Rumors spread and people became panic stricken: bands of brigands—groups of violent ruffians—supposedly paid by aristocrats to wreak bloody vengeance on the Third Estate were reported to be approaching, burning crops, killing people, destroying whole towns. Austrian troops, or British marines, or Spanish troops—all murdering, pillaging mercenaries hired by aristocrats—were supposedly massed for invasion and would arrive within the hour. Fear approached hysteria, and despite the lack of any evidence for these threats, panicked peasants armed themselves with pitchforks and scythes for defense.

The Great Fear ended as abruptly as it began. But when the brigands and invading troops failed to materialize anywhere in France, the peasants did not put down their weapons. They continued rioting.

It is still unclear just why the Great Fear swept the countryside with such ferocity, completely passing over some districts, raging furiously in others. However, the violence was clearly alarming to the bourgeoisie in the towns and especially to the deputies at the National Assembly in

An Incident of Hysteria

In a journal excerpt quoted in Blood Sisters *by Marilyn Yalom, the Marquise de La Tour du Pin describes an incident of the Great Fear hysteria while she was visiting in the province of Normandy.*

"Women were crying and lamenting, angry men were swearing and menacing. Others raised their hands to the sky crying out: 'We are lost!' In their midst, a man on horseback was making a speech. . . . 'They'll be here in three hours, they're pillaging in Gaillefontaines, they're setting the barns on fire, etc. etc.'. . .

Since I am not easily frightened, I went down. I mounted my horse and started to trot through the street where little by little a crowd of people gathered who thought their last day had arrived. I spoke out, trying to persuade them that there wasn't a single word of truth in anything they had heard."

Versailles. The National Assembly knew it had to restore order if it hoped to achieve a new, stable government in France.

"They Have All Gone Quite Mad"

Deputies agreed that concessions to the people on feudal rents and privileges must be made in order to stop the violence. A group of liberal nobles decided on a plan. They would renounce in a meeting of the assembly the feudal rents against which the peasants were protesting and hope that other nobles would follow. They chose as their leader the Duke d'Aiguillon, one of France's wealthiest landowners. The meeting was set for the evening of August 4.

Events went as planned. The deputies responded with enthusiasm to the Duke d'Aiguillon's speech, and one after another stood up to renounce their privileges. As emotions escalated, other privileges were given up as well: not just feudal rents and fees were renounced, but the rights to hunting, to sale of offices, to keeping pigeons; even the clergy renounced rights to tithes. This "contagion of sentimental feeling," as one observer called it, went on until two in the morning. The renunciation of rights flowed so quickly from so many deputies that the assembly's clerks could not write fast enough to record it all. One of the conservative deputies was so annoyed at the proceedings that he passed a note to the president: "Suspend the session. They have all gone quite mad."[36]

However, the sober light of day washed away some of the night's emotion, and over the next few days some sacrifices were modified. Nevertheless, by the morn-

The Declaration of the Rights of Man and the Citizen ended the ancien régime and granted rights to the common people of France.

ing of August 5, the ancien régime had almost entirely disappeared.

With the old feudal system swept away, the way was opened for a new constitution. Many deputies believed that the constitution should be based on a declaration of rights. As the deputy Mounier argued:

> For a constitution to be a good one, it must be based on the rights of man and must protect these rights; we must understand the rights which are granted to all men by natural justice, we must recall all the principles which are at the base of any human society.[37]

The first important idea in the document was that "men are born and remain free and equal in rights." Those rights included freedom of speech, equality under the law, and freedom to own property. No longer would certain classes of people enjoy special privileges. All the people, whether commoner or noble, would be treated the same. A second important principle of the document was the notion that sovereignty was with the people, not the king. The absolutism of kings was completely dismissed.

The October Days

Finally, after much debate, the Declaration of the Rights of Man and of the Citizen was adopted by the National Assembly on August 26, 1789. However, the king was not willing to approve either the reforms of August 4 or the new declaration. "I will never consent to the spoilation of my clergy or my nobility," he declared, "and I will not sanction decrees which seek to despoil them."[38]

In Paris, patriots, revolutionary pamphleteers, and members of the Paris Commune feared that the king might try to reverse the reforms. Some believed that the king should take up residence in Paris, where the revolutionaries could influence his decisions. As the bread shortages worsened, pamphleteers took advantage of the situation by blaming aristocrats for withholding grain, hoping to anger the people and force the king to Paris, away from the influence of court aristocrats. In the meantime, the king, alarmed at the continuing agitation, summoned troops to Versailles. The Flanders Regiment arrived on September 29. As was the custom, upon their arrival a banquet was given in their honor. The soldiers became rowdy with too much wine, and when the king and queen appeared, soldiers greeted them with cheers and pledges of loyalty. The band struck up a royalist tune. Soldiers tore the revolutionary tricolor cockades from their hats, trampled them, and made insulting remarks about the National Assembly.

When news of the banquet reached Paris a few days later, people were outraged. Counterrevolutionaries were banqueting at Versailles while the poor of Paris starved. This appeared to be just the event that the radical revolutionaries and patriots were waiting for.

On October 5, about 9 A.M., a rough and angry crowd of working women from the poor sections gathered at city hall de-

Women march to Versailles to ask the king for bread. The crowd gathered force, eventually comprising as many as six thousand people.

France in Chaos

Throughout September 1789, France was in a state of near chaos. The king had refused to agree to the assembly's reforms, while the delegates quarreled among themselves. Throughout the country there were food shortages and general unrest, and in Paris members of the commune had taken over the Paris government, while political agitators stirred up the people. In a letter home quoted in English Witnesses of the French Revolution, *edited by J. M. Thompson, British ambassador William Eden describes the state of affairs.*

"The plan of a Constitution recommended by the Committee of the National Assembly . . . would probably have [brought] a period of tranquillity, and would have allowed the entering upon the great work of providing for the debt and deficit, both of which in the present state of things are increasing every hour: but the Assembly is ill-circumstanced in all respects. The [nobility and clergy] cannot bring themselves to wish cordially for any result which, however necessary to the Kingdom for the sake of its internal tranquillity, may sanctify the violences done to their respective classes; and the representatives of the [Third Estate], considered collectively, are factious, ignorant, and absurd. There are in all the Orders some individuals of great integrity, right meaning, and good talents, but in general they are under intimidation from the lower people of Paris and of the chief Provincial Towns, and there is not yet any man who stands forward with talents and weight to guide the others: In effect the Kingdom of France is at this hour governed by some nameless individuals who assemble every morning and evening at the Hotel de Ville Paris. The Court of Versailles is not only in appearance but in fact in a state of imprisonment. The nominal Ministers of the Country avow without reserve that they are merely nominal. The Church is not only without influence but without respect, and is soon likely to be without bread. The Army is without discipline and almost without soldiers. The treasury is without money, and nearly without credit . . . and lastly the Magistracy is without power or functions."

manding bread. They stormed into the building, disarming guards and collecting weapons. When they were told that the commune could not help them and that they would have to see the king, they set off for Versailles, joined by a number of men sympathetic to their cause. Other women fell in with them along the way. Many of the new recruits carried heavy sticks, scythes, pikes, pitchforks, and knives. Soon the crowd was six thousand strong. Political agitators were quick to take advantage of the situation and joined the crowd, disguising themselves as women. Their hope was to force the king to sanction the assembly's decrees and to move to Paris. As they marched to Versailles it began to rain. The group continued slogging through mud and rain all afternoon, reaching Versailles and the assembly hall about 5:30 that afternoon.

When news of the march of the marketwomen spread through Paris, hundreds of national guardsmen appeared at city hall demanding that Lafayette lead them to Versailles to bring the king back to Paris. Lafayette was reluctant, but his guards insisted, threatening to hang him from a lantern post if he refused. Finally, toward evening, National Guard troops marched out of Paris toward Versailles, with Lafayette at their head.

A Demand to the King

At just about the time Lafayette left Paris, the women were pouring into the assembly hall to demand bread. The business of the assembly came to a halt as the rowdy women occupied the public galleries, hanging their wet stockings and skirts over the railing to dry, using foul language, shouting at the deputies, and demanding bread. Finally the assembly suggested sending a delegation of women to the king. The king graciously received the women, who explained their purpose. In his most charming manner, he immediately replied, "You know my heart. I will order all the bread in Versailles to be collected and given to you."[39]

Shortly before midnight, Lafayette and twenty thousand National Guard arrived at Versailles, tired, cold, mud spattered. He immediately visited the king and explained that he had come to take the king to Paris. The king agreed to sleep on the decision after a promise from Lafayette that his troops would protect the royal family.

Just before dawn, a mob of women entered the palace through an unlocked gate, determined to find the queen and murder her. The queen's guards tried to stop them, but were overpowered. Two of the guards were killed. The women reached the queen's rooms, and the queen fled in her nightclothes to the king's apartments. Finally, Lafayette's guards cleared

Bread rioters take over the Hall of the Constitution, carrying the heads of murdered guards on pikes.

out the intruders, but outside the mob paraded in the courtyard, carrying the heads of the murdered guards on pikes, shouting "The king to Paris!"

That afternoon a coach left Versailles carrying the royal family. The National Guard led the way, followed by the royal coach with Lafayette riding beside it. The royal coach was surrounded by disorderly crowds of women shouting insults at the queen. They also bore the same bloody trophies of the night before on pikes, as one eyewitness, Victorine de Chastenay, recounts:

> The odious multitude finally started off to Paris. Some of them carried several loaves of bread stuck on their spears or bayonets; but what was most unbelievable is that the heads of the Queen's guards preceded them.[40]

Throughout the six-hour march back to Paris, the women chanted, "We have the baker, and the baker's wife, and the baker's boy—now we shall have bread!"

That evening the royal family was taken to the Tuileries, a palace in the center of Paris that had not been occupied for over a century. "It's very ugly," complained the king's young son, the dauphin. But neither he nor his parents would ever again occupy the magnificent palace at Versailles.

5 Making a New Nation

The people had their way—the king was in Paris and the assembly, for the most part, had followed. It seemed that the summer's upheavals had died down. The season's grain harvest had been plentiful, and the bread crisis was easing. The assembly, installed in a meeting hall called the Manège, an old riding school just behind the Tuileries, was ready to get on with the business of a new constitution. However, the Revolution was not over; new forces began stirring as the revolutionaries divided themselves into opposing factions.

The Right, the Left, and the Center

France lacked political parties as we know them today; nevertheless, even before the assembly moved to Paris, the deputies had begun to separate themselves according to their political interests.

The smallest group was the conservatives, known as the monarchists or royalists, who supported the king and were opposed to the reforms of August 4. They wanted to stop the Revolution and to maintain the rights and privileges of the aristocracy. Many of the monarchists,

alarmed at the violence and growing power of the extreme revolutionaries, resigned from the assembly when it left Versailles, and some fled the country, joining the growing ranks of émigrés. The few who were left took their seats to the right of the president in the assembly hall at Paris.

To the president's left sat a group who felt that the Revolution had not gone far enough. They were interested in the rights of the common people and wanted a democratic form of government in which all people, not just property owners, had the right to vote.

The largest group, seated in the center, was composed of moderately liberal deputies who wanted a constitutional monarchy in which the king retained some power and the assembly made the laws. This group included men such as Lafayette, Mirabeau, and the Abbé Sièyes.

As these men took their seats in the assembly hall, they could not know that their seating arrangements gave rise to the political terms we use today: the left, or liberal thinkers, and the right, or conservative thinkers.

Deputies within these three main groups were not all of one mind. Gradually, their differences crystallized and alliances shifted. Political clubs formed

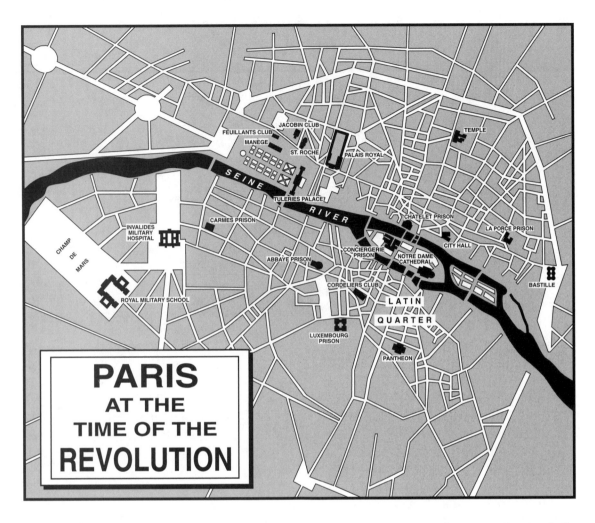

PARIS
AT THE
TIME OF THE
REVOLUTION

where deputies and citizens of like mind met to air their political views and to discuss their plans for the new government.

Jacobins and Cordeliers

The most important club was called the Jacobins, named after a Dominican monastery in which they held their meetings. (In France, the Dominicans were known as Jacobins.) At first only assembly deputies were members, but later non-deputies who could afford the expensive annual dues were allowed to join. In their early days, the Jacobins were moderate liberals and included Lafayette as a member. By 1791 the Jacobins had come under the influence of the more radical Maximilien Robespierre, and Lafayette left to form a more moderate group known as the Feuillants. However, Jacobin clubs remained the most popular, and spread throughout the provinces. The Jacobins soon became the most powerful force in the assembly. Arthur Young, an English traveler to France, gives his impressions after attending a meeting of the Jacobins:

Political radical Maximilien Robespierre (near left) led the influential Jacobins (far left).

In this club the business that is to be brought into the National Assembly is regularly debated; the motions are read that are intended to be made there and rejected . . . or approved. When these have been fully agreed to, the whole party are engaged to support them. . . . And I may add that . . . whatever passes in this club is almost sure to pass in the assembly.[41]

Thus the Jacobins had enormous influence in the assembly. And later, as events unfolded under the leadership of Robespierre, the name "Jacobin" became the most feared name of the Revolution.

The expensive dues of the Jacobin clubs excluded the working class, who, determined to take part in politics, formed their own club, the Cordeliers. This club, while made up of sansculotte—workers, businessmen, and artisans—attracted leaders and spokesmen such as the well-educated lawyer Georges Danton, and the wild, radical journalist, Jean-Paul Marat

(men who would soon become important figures of the Revolution), and Camille Desmoulins, who had urged the crowd at the Palais Royal to take up arms.

Despite their political differences, National Assembly deputies moved forward with the work of the Revolution in the relatively peaceful year of 1790.

A New Administration

Deputies continued drafting the new constitution. Although the constitution was not completed and accepted until 1791, many of its reforms were rapidly put into effect. A practical and long-lasting achievement of the assembly was reorganizing the ancien régime's administration. The nation was divided into eighty-three subdivisions, or departments. Under the reforms, the local officials were not appointed by the king, but were elected.

The judicial system was reformed. Judges were elected. There was no more buying justice by bribing judges. Torture as an instrument of law was abolished. Under the ancien régime, the king had the power to imprison citizens whether or not there was evidence of crime. Under the new reforms, people were guaranteed trials by jury. Sentences were more merciful, with the death penalty reserved for only the most serious offenses.

While these reforms marked a great step forward for the French, some citizens were still left out of the process. Most of the deputies were bourgeoisie who were reluctant to give equality to all citizens. Only those citizens who paid taxes valued at three days' wages could vote; only landowners could hold public office. The poor peasants and workers were excluded; it was still a revolution for the benefit of the bourgeoisie. Thus, while liberty was guaranteed to all, the promise of equality remained unfulfilled. Nevertheless, people were filled with great hope as a new spirit of national solidarity arose.

Festival of the Federation

On July 14, 1790, one year after the fall of the Bastille, France held a great festival. Across the country, in the spirit of new national pride, towns and municipalities had formed federations, or agreements of friendship, among themselves. Detachments of the provincial National Guard, popularly called *fédérés*, converged on Paris to celebrate patriotic unity, the fall of the Bastille, and all that implied—freedom and a new constitutional government.

For weeks beforehand, thousands of Parisian workmen dug up the huge public square, the Champ de Mars, building an amphitheater. When the date of the celebration neared and the work was not complete, citizens pitched in to finish the job.

A meeting of the Jacobin Club. The high dues demanded of members prevented the common people from joining.

Three hundred thousand people gather to celebrate the fall of the Bastille and the ancien régime at the Festival of the Federation.

On July 14, steady rain did not stop three hundred thousand people from taking their places to view the spectacle, which began with an impressive procession of assembly deputies, followed by the royal family, marching solemnly between rows of brightly colored flags. Lafayette rode at the head of his National Guard in their brilliant blue coats. Fourteen thousand *fédérés* from the provinces followed, carrying eighty-three banners representing the eighty-three departments.

At the Altar of the Nation in the center of the amphitheater, Charles-Maurice de Talleyrand-Périgord, bishop of Autun and deputy of the assembly, said mass attended by three hundred priests wearing the tricolor scarves. Talleyrand blessed the eighty-three banners, and then Lafayette led the National Guard to the altar to take an oath of loyalty to the nation. Finally,

the king stood up and a solemn silence fell over the crowd: "I, King of the French, swear to employ the power delegated to me in maintaining the constitution decreed by the National Assembly and accepted by me."[42]

Thousands of voices went up in a great shout *"Vive le Roi!"* People celebrated for several days with fireworks, banquets, balls, and parades.

Reforming the Church

Meanwhile, the debates in the assembly continued as the economy grew even worse. Peasants, emboldened by their weapons and the spirit of reform, refused to pay taxes, and Necker was forced to borrow even more money. Finally, Bishop

Talleyrand offered a solution. Talleyrand had been forced by his aristocratic family to enter the clergy, but he became an avid anticleric. Thus it was no surprise when he suggested that France take over church property and sell it to pay the national debt. With the help of Jacobin deputies, the idea was accepted by the assembly. Paper bills called assignats were issued for the people to use to purchase confiscated church property. These assignats quickly became currency. In return for church land, the assembly agreed to take over some church responsibilities such as education, public charity, and paying salaries to priests. High-ranking clergy protested loudly, but it was useless.

The assembly soon realized that, with the confiscation of church lands, they needed to reorganize the church in France. The most controversial of the religious reforms was the Civil Constitution of the Clergy. Adopted on July 12, 1790, just two days before the Festival of the Federation, the Civil Constitution provided that bishops and priests be elected by the people, and that the French church answer to the government, not to the pope in Rome. In Roman Catholicism, the pope is the supreme authority of the church in every country, but the assembly was determined to make the church subject to the state. Deputies argued that since the state now paid the clergy's salaries, people should have the right to elect them, and the pope should have no power over French church affairs. As one supporter of the reform, Armand Camus, claimed:

A Fervor of Building

Parisians of all classes were caught up in the fervor of the preparations for the Festival of the Federation. In her memoirs, quoted in Blood Sisters *by Marilyn Yalom, Madame de Tourzel, governess of the royal children, describes the rush to complete the amphitheater in the Champ de Mars.*

"Everyone wanted to have a part of the action. . . . Even the ladies had themselves driven there in carriages so they could help fill the wheelbarrows; and everyone who might have passed quietly by the Champ de Mars without stopping ran the risk of being insulted. . . .

There were workers, bourgeois men and women, Carthusian monks and others from different orders, military men, beautiful ladies, men and women from every class and all stations of society. . . . From time to time one heard the repeated cries of 'Long live the Nation! Aristocrats to the lantern-posts!' and . . . patriotic hymns by ladies impassioned of the Revolution. Several of them, even from the highest social class, became so fatigued that they fell sick, and finished by being victims of their patriotic zeal."

What is the Pope? The Pope is a bishop, the minister of Jesus Christ, just like any other. . . . It is high time that the Church of France . . . should be freed from this servitude.[43]

When they passed the measure, deputies did not foresee the storm it would cause throughout the country. France was still a deeply religious country, a Catholic country, and many were not willing to give up that heritage. A number of French bishops appealed to the pope to take a stand against the measure. But the pope hesitated, and in the meantime, on November 27, the assembly decreed that all clergy must take an oath supporting the Civil

Charles Maurice de Talleyrand-Périgord suggested that all church property be seized and sold to pay for the enormous foreign debt of the French government.

Constitution of the Clergy. In the oath, clergy pledged "to be loyal to the nation, the law and the king, and to uphold . . . the constitution." Thus their first loyalty was to France, not to the church or to the pope. Half the clergy of France refused to take the oath. In many areas peasants supported their local priests' refusal to take the oath. In other areas, priests who refused to take the oath were threatened. When the pope finally announced that he opposed the measure and ordered those clergy who had taken the oath to retract it, the divisions grew deeper.

The Civil Constitution of the Clergy provided fuel to the counterrevolutionaries who opposed the Revolution and wanted a return to the old ways. Throughout the country, people who had once supported the Revolution changed sides, believing the assembly had gone too far. As one historian noted, "The Civil Constitution was not just another piece of institutional legislation. It was the beginning of a holy war."[44]

Émigrés and Counter-revolutionaries

Monarchs, aristocrats, and liberals throughout Europe had watched the progress of the Revolution closely. In 1789, it was cheered by many liberal thinkers who hoped for the same kinds of reforms in their own country, but that admiration did not last long. When the ancien régime and feudal privileges were abolished, aristocratic classes throughout Europe turned against the Revolution; when church property was confiscated and the Civil Constitution of the Clergy was passed, European

Refractory Priests

Priests who refused to take the oath supporting the Civil Constitution of the Clergy were called "refractory priests" or "refractories." Often these priests preached against the Revolution. In his history The French Revolution 1787-1799, *professor Albert Soboul describes the effect these refractories had in France.*

"The agitation of the refractories gave new inspiration to the counter-revolutionary opposition. They linked their cause to that of the nobles and chose to become the active agents of counter-revolution, continuing to practise their religion and to administer the sacraments. The country divided. Many people were unwilling to risk their eternal salvation by abandoning the [good fathers] in their moment of crisis, and hence the refractories succeeded in their attempt to lead part of the population into the ranks of the counter-revolutionary opposition. Disorders grew more violent till, on 7 May 1791, the [assembly] authorized the conduct of religious services by the refractories in the same way as they permitted other religious bodies to conduct public worship. The constitutional clergy, however, [those clergy who had taken the oath] became extremely angry at this concession, for they were afraid that they would be unable to stand up to the competition of the refractories. Religious war broke out in France."

clergy turned against the Revolution. Middle-class Europeans were disturbed as well, frightened by the turmoil and the often brutal violence of the peasants and Parisian sansculotte. As the French Revolution wore on, Europeans of all classes feared that revolution would spread to their own countries. Political reaction set in, urged on by the émigrés who hoped to enlist military support to recapture their country and their privileged positions.

As hostility to the Revolution grew, some European monarchs took action. Spain placed troops along its border to halt what it called "the French plague." In Prussia, an army was being organized for the "crusade." Although some monarchs were cautious about intervening, many were as enthusiastic as Catherine II of Russia, who claimed, "To destroy the anarchy that reigns in France is to prepare one's immortal glory."[45]

It was in this atmosphere that one of the key events of the Revolution took place.

The Flight to Varennes

Held as a virtual hostage at the Tuileries, the king realized that he was nearly power-

A CORDÉE A M.
50 MILLE LIVRE
20 MILLE LIVRE

Louis XVI's elaborate plans to escape from Paris across the border into Austria failed miserably.

less. He was constantly urged by his advisers and by the queen to flee. His hesitation was resolved when the Civil Constitution of the Clergy was passed by the assembly. Urged on by events at home and counterrevolutionaries abroad, the king took action.

On the morning of June 21, 1791, the king's valet went to the king's bedchamber to awaken him. The valet found the bed empty. The king had escaped during the night. A search of the Tuileries revealed that the entire royal family was gone, despite the hundreds of national guardsmen who patrolled the palace and sentinels who stood watch at each gate. An alarm was raised. Deputies rushed to the Manège. Now that the king was no longer under the watchful eye of the assembly—perhaps no longer in France—deputies feared invasion by foreign armies on the borders.

The royal family were on their way to the frontier, where a contingent of royalist soldiers waited to escort them to safety across the border, where both the king's brother-in-law, the Austrian emperor, and the king of Spain might be able to help reverse the Revolution and restore the king to power.

Intricate plans had been in preparation for weeks. The royal family would travel disguised as a party of foreign travelers. The children's governess carried a forged passport in the name of Baroness von Korff, and the young dauphin was disguised in a girl's dress and bonnet. However, the plan went awry. The carriage in which they were traveling was heavily loaded, slowing down the horses. After waiting four hours, their escort gave up hope and left. When the coach finally did arrive, there was no escort, and the fugitives had to press on alone. When the royal coach arrived at the town of Varennes, suspicious citizens held up the coach and notified Paris. The royal family were forced to await the arrival of National Guard troops sent from Paris on order of Lafayette to escort them back to the Tuileries. The National Guard commander handed the king the paper authorizing the royal family's forced return to Paris. After reading it, the king commented sadly, "There is no longer a king in France."

The trip back to Paris was a hot, miserable, five-day ordeal. When the royal family finally arrived, they were met by immense crowds. Streets were lined with the National Guard with their weapons held in reverse position as was the custom for funerals, and the crowds were strangely quiet. According to Madame de Tourzel, the children's governess, people did not remove their hats, a customary sign of respect:

> Following the order of Monsieur de Lafayette, everyone had his head covered; he had also enjoined them to remain absolutely silent to show the King, he said, the feelings his trip had inspired. His orders were so strictly ob-

served that several scullery-boys without hats covered their heads with their dirty, filthy handkerchiefs.[46]

Thus the king returned to Paris as a prisoner in disgrace, and in the eyes of many, a traitor.

The Sansculotte and the Champ de Mars Massacre

Many citizens welcomed the king's flight. "At last we are free and without a King," claimed the Cordeliers.[47] Louis had betrayed their trust, and they felt they no longer owed him allegiance. Sansculotte, members of the Cordeliers Club, and some radical members of the Jacobins pushed for a republican form of government that excluded the king altogether, a government in which all men, whether taxpayers or not, had the right to vote.

Louis XVI and family arrive under heavy guard at the Hôtel de Ville on July 17, 1789. Many labeled the king a traitor.

The assembly, made up of a majority of middle-class landowners and businessmen, was afraid that the counterrevolutionary forces poised on the borders, with spies working within the country, could turn back the Revolution, restoring the king and the privileges of aristocracy. On the other hand, the assembly feared even more the peasants and the working classes, the sansculotte, whom they viewed as a violent, unruly rabble and as serious a danger to property as was the counterrevolution.

What, then, to do with the king? Finally, over the objections of Robespierre and other radical members of the assembly, the king was absolved from responsibility; he was found innocent of treason

After his failed flight to Varennes, Louis XVI returned to Paris in disgrace as a prisoner. The assembly's decision to declare the king innocent of treason created even more tension between the workers and the well-to-do middle class.

on condition that he accept the completed version of the constitution.

The assembly's action toward the king added to the growing rift between the workers and the well-to-do middle class. The sansculotte, spurred on by Cordelier propaganda, were determined to petition for republican government. Three days after the second anniversary of the storming of the Bastille, July 17, 1791, a petition was placed on the Altar of the Nation in the Champ de Mars, where people of the city could come to sign it. As crowds lined up to sign the petition, two men were discovered hiding under the steps leading up to the altar. No one knows for sure what the two men were doing, but the crowd was convinced they were spies, and immediately hauled them off to be hanged from a lantern post.

News reached city hall of the unruly crowd. The mayor called out the National Guard. Led by Lafayette, the guard contingent reached the Champ de Mars square, where an angry mob of fifty thousand greeted them by throwing stones. Lafayette ordered the crowd to disperse but they continued threatening the guard. Finally, Lafayette gave the order to fire. When the crowd finally fled before the guardsmen's musket fire, nearly fifty people were dead.

Law and Order Restored

The incident made clear to everyone that the growing rift between the moderate bourgeoisie, who wanted to maintain a constitutional monarchy, and those who wanted republican government could not be mended. Both groups viewed the aris-

Better Off Without a King

The American Revolution pamphleteer Thomas Paine was a visitor to Paris when the king attempted to escape. In English Witnesses of the French Revolution, *editor J. M. Thompson quotes Paine's "Republican Manifesto" in which Paine explains why the nation was better off without the king.*

"The serene tranquillity, the mutual confidence which prevailed amongst us during the time of the King's escape, the indifference with which we beheld him return, are unequivocal proofs that the absence of a King is more desirable than his presence, and that he is not only a political superfluity, but a grievous burden, pressing hard on the whole nation. . . .

He has abdicated the throne in having fled from his post. Abdication and desertion are not characterized by the length of absence; but by the single act of flight. In the present instance, the act is everything, and the time nothing.

The nation can never give back its confidence to a man who, false to his trust, perjured to his oath, conspires a [secret] flight, obtains a fraudulent passport . . . [flees] to a frontier covered with traitors and deserters, and evidently meditates a return into our country, with a force capable of imposing his own despotic laws. . . . He holds no longer any authority. We owe him no longer obedience."

tocracy and counterrevolutionaries as common enemies—but they increasingly viewed each other as enemies as well. Following the incident, the moderate assembly ordered many radicals arrested and closed the Cordeliers Club. Thus, for the short term at least, the moderates in the assembly maintained the upper hand. Law and order was restored to Paris.

On September 3, 1791, the assembly approved the final draft of the constitution, and Louis approved it on September 14. On the following day he again took an oath to uphold the new constitution. Their work done, the assembly disbanded on September 30, not knowing that within a year their work would be swept away in another wave of revolution.

6 The Widening War and the New Revolution

Enemies of the Revolution were everywhere: émigré spies, counterrevolutionaries, royalists, refractory priests. Worse yet, France was surrounded by hostile foreign powers encouraged by aristocratic émigrés, with armies poised on the borders. On August 27, 1791, Austria and Prussia signed the Declaration of Pillnitz, which stated that they would "act promptly, by common consent and with such force as might be needed" to restore the French monarchy to its rightful place.[48] War seemed inevitable.

On top of these troubles, the assignat, the paper money, was falling in value, causing food prices to rise. There was a shortage of food and other necessities such as soap. Food riots began to break out once again.

These were the conditions that faced the new deputies of the Legislative Assembly, which met for the first time on October 1, 1791.

Girondins, Jacobins, and Feuillants

According to the constitution, the deputies of the National Assembly were prohibited from serving in the new Legislative Assembly. The new assembly deputies were solidly middle class. Most were young and unknown, and many had experience in politics at the local government level. One group in particular stood out—young men from the province of Gironde. These men, members of the Jacobin Club, frequently met at the home of Jean-Marie Roland, a man of mediocre talents, much older than his lovely, vibrant, intelligent wife, Manon Roland. She became the moving spirit of this new group, although a silent one as she describes in her memoirs:

> I knew what role was appropriate for my sex, and I never abandoned it. The meetings took place in my presence without my taking any part in them. Placed outside the circle near a table, I worked with my hands or wrote letters, while they deliberated. But . . . I did not lose a word of what was uttered, and sometimes I had to bite my lips so as not to say a word of my own.[49]

These young Jacobins soon became known as Girondins, and, along with other members of the Jacobin Club, made up the left wing of the new Legislative Assembly. The Girondins were intense idealists who took the writings of philosopher Rousseau as their guiding principle, and who fancied themselves as inheritors of the ideals of the ancient Roman republic. This group of men were the most gifted in the new assembly, and the most fiery, effective orators. Unfortunately, they were not skilled at putting their ideals into practice.

Before the Champ de Mars incident, many Jacobins, including Lafayette, had left the club and joined the Feuillants. These conservatives and moderates made up the right wing in the new assembly. They favored a limited monarchy and were strongly opposed to both the ancien régime and the movement toward democracy.

In the center of the new assembly sat the bulk of delegates, who were somewhere between the two groups. They supported the constitution, but lacked strong political ideals and had no outstanding leaders. Thus, despite their limited numbers, the brilliant oratory of the Girondins carried the greatest weight.

"Through Blood Alone"

Despite the growing food crisis and worsening economic conditions, the Legislative Assembly turned its attention to the counterrevolutionaries. Never mind the day-to-day practical problems of running a country; the Girondins in the assembly were more interested in revolutionary ideals.

The Girondins, led by Jacques Brissot, began to demand war against those nations who harbored émigrés and who threatened France. "The moment has come for a new crusade, a crusade for universal liberty," he declared.[50] Outside the assembly meeting, Brissot's fiery speech was echoed by Madame Roland: "Peace

Manon Roland witnessed the meetings of the Jacobin Club in her home, but, in keeping with her gender, never participated in them.

will set us back. . . . We can be regenerated through blood alone."[51]

The Girondins and the king agreed on war, yet for very different reasons. Secretly, the king was hoping war would force the counterrevolutionaries to rally around him and restore him to his old position of power. The Girondins wanted to expand their revolutionary ideals to nations beyond France, and they also knew that war abroad would solidify the people behind the new government. The people, still in fear of the very real threats on their borders, were easily convinced. But Robespierre argued urgently against the war. The two Jacobins, Brissot and Robespierre, heatedly debated the issue. Their

Fearing the penetration of France by Austria, the Girondins (pictured here) strongly supported war. The king voted with the Girondins.

disagreement would split the revolutionary group permanently, as the Girondins became a political force separate from the Jacobins. Robespierre rightly judged the king's motives in agreeing to war. He also realized that if war ended in victory, an ambitious general might seize power. Robespierre was farsighted and courageous, but public opinion and Girondin eloquence won the day. On April 20, 1792, the king appeared before the assembly to formally declare war on Austria.

The war did not go as planned by the Girondins. The French army was ill-prepared for the conflict and met disaster almost immediately. As they crossed the Belgian frontier and caught sight of the enemy, their generals, lacking confidence in the army, ordered retreat. The soldiers, believing they were betrayed, hanged one of the generals. People immediately blamed traitors within and without the nation for the disastrous beginning to the war.

The war, begun so hastily and with so little preparation, was the force that started the next great wave of the revolutionary movement.

"Down with the Veto"

Spring brought no relief to the poor's economic hardships. When news of the army's disastrous retreat reached the people, they became even more convinced that they were the victims of counterrevolutionaries, and they blamed the Girondins for their problems. Girondins tried to regain the support of the people: They passed a decree levying a severe penalty on refractory priests and they decreed that a force of twenty thousand national guardsmen be stationed outside Paris to protect the city. The king vetoed the decrees by the power granted to him under the new constitution. Divisions among political factions grew deeper. Girondins accused Jacobins, who opposed the war, of being counterrevolutionaries; Jacobins accused Girondins of being agents of the court; the journalist Marat attacked both sides, urging soldiers to kill their officers.

The sansculotte, disgusted at the way the assembly was handling matters, took action on their own. On June 10, 1792, a crowd of eight thousand Parisian citizens armed with pitchforks and pikes descended on the Tuileries palace, shouting

The "Accursed Revolution"

A young Englishman, William Cobbett, visited France from March to September 1792, and later wrote about his impressions of the "accursed revolution" during that time. An excerpt from his letter is quoted by editor J. M. Thompson in English Witnesses of the French Revolution.

"I arrived in France in March 1792 and continued there till the beginning of September following, the six happiest months of my life. I should be a most ungrateful monster that ever existed, were I to speak ill of the French people in general. I went to that country full of all those prejudices that Englishmen suck in with their mother's milk against the French, and against their religion: a few weeks convinced me that I had been deceived with respect to both. I met everywhere with civility, and even hospitality, in a degree that I had never been accustomed to. I found the people among whom I lived, excepting those who were already blasted with the principles of the accursed revolution, honest, pious, and kind to excess. People may say what they please about the misery of the French peasantry under the old government: I have conversed with thousands of them, [and there were not ten of them] who did not regret the change. . . . I did intend to stay in France till the spring of 1793. . . . But I perceived the storm gathering; I saw that a war with England was inevitable; and it was not difficult to see what would be the fate of Englishmen in that country, where the rulers had laid aside even the appearance of justice and mercy. I wished, however, to see Paris. . . . I was even on the way, when I heard at Abbeville that the King was dethroned, and his guards murdered. This intelligence made me turn off towards Havre-le-Grace, whence I embarked for America."

"Down with the Veto." The riotous crowd broke into the building and located the king. They forced him to put on a red cap, a mark of the revolutionary sansculotte, and forced him to drink to the health of the nation. The king quietly complied with the crowd's wishes. "People of Paris, I drink to your health and to that of the French nation," he said, drinking the wine handed him.[52] But he refused to change his mind on the vetoes. Finally, the crowd was cleared from the building.

Many people were sympathetic to the king when they heard how he had maintained his courage in the midst of humiliation. In Paris, over twenty thousand people signed a petition protesting the demonstration against the king. Meanwhile the sansculotte were beginning to feel their own power: They wanted the assembly to depose the king and declare a republic. The Girondins had their backs against the wall. They were being threatened by the radical revolutionaries in Paris, and the war was going badly, with Austrian troops ready to cross the border into France. Lafayette, disgusted with the way the Revolution was going, had deserted to the Austrians. Realizing the danger from Austria, Jacobins and Girondins declared a momentary truce in their quarrel. On July 11, the assembly, led by Brissot, declared a state of emergency:

> Large concentrations of troops are advancing on our frontiers, and all those who regard liberty with horror are taking up arms to destroy our Constitution. Citizens! *La Patrie est en danger!* [The nation is in danger!][53]

The sansculotte enter the Palace of the Tuileries. Many people protested their public humiliation of the king, and they fell from popularity.

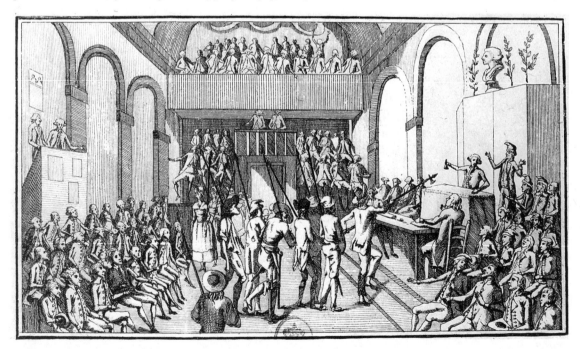

Sansculotte threaten and humiliate King Louis XVI, forcing him to wear the red cap of a revolutionary.

Paris was soon overflowing with *fédérés*, many of whom were republicans and were warmly welcomed as heroes by the Parisian sansculotte. However, many citizens found the rough *fédérés* from the provinces "an infernal gang of assassins."

The Sansculotte Take Charge

During the following weeks, events proceeded quickly. Petitions to depose the king were circulating through nearly all the forty-eight sections of Paris. The war news grew more alarming. The Duke of Brunswick, commander of the enemy army, issued a warning that he would invade and destroy Paris if the royal family were harmed. One of the Paris districts issued a decree doing away with the distinctions between "active" citizens who could afford to pay taxes—and thus vote—and "passive" citizens who could not pay taxes. Thus full equality of all citizens was recognized, which marked the coming of democracy into the Revolution. Alarmed at the threat of invasion, the Paris Commune ordered that all citizens who were armed be enlisted in the National Guard. Soon the guard looked more like an army of sansculotte than a well-armed, well-mannered bourgeois force.

Soon, officials of the Paris sections began to act independently of the Paris Commune at city hall, where the Girondin mayor Jérôme Pétion governed. The Cordeliers, led by Georges Danton, encouraged the sansculotte and the *fédérés* to call for an uprising and assisted in giving out weapons and ammunition. One Paris section announced that if the assembly did not depose the king by August 9, it

The assembly called all the National Guard troops throughout the country to arms. Responding to the urgent call, *fédérés* from the provinces converged on Paris by the hundreds. One group from the southern province of Marseilles marched to Paris singing a rousingly patriotic new song which became known as "The Marseillaise," and which would one day become the French national anthem.

Armed with muskets and pikes, volunteers gather in Paris to help defend their country from the Austrian troops about to cross the border into France.

would take action. About thirty other sections joined the action, and a revolutionary municipal assembly was formed with delegates from each section. All Paris knew that a crisis was at hand.

The Revolution of August 10

On the night of August 9, the delegates from the revolutionary assembly arrived at city hall and unlawfully took over the city government, disbanding the Paris Commune and replacing it with their own Insurrectionary Commune. Unlike the middle-class lawyers and businessmen who made up the Paris Commune, the Insurrectionary Commune was made up primarily of artisans, who were true representatives of the sansculotte.

The Paris night of August 9, 1792, was hot, almost tropical, and heavy with suspense. At the Tuileries, all the windows were open and the palace was ablaze with candles. In the royal apartments on the second floor, the king and his family were gathered.

Throughout the rest of the palace, the king's passionately loyal nine hundred Swiss guards made preparations for defense. In the courtyard facing the palace, some two thousand national guardsmen were in place to protect the Tuileries, but the guardsmen were in sympathy with the citizens. Before morning, the guard had turned the cannon around to face the Tuileries.

With the royal family was Pierre-Louis Roederer, a representative of the Department of Paris. Just at dawn, they began to hear news that huge crowds were gathering in the sections. Realizing that there was

10 August 1792

The August 10 attack on the Tuileries was not just another incidence of mob violence. It was also the beginning of a new era and the end of liberal government. In his book The French Revolution, *historian J. F. Bosher explains the significance of the August 10 revolution.*

"The revolution of 10 August 1792, which brought down the constitutional monarchy, was not merely an advanced stage of the Revolution that had broken out in June 1789. It was quite different and brought changes as profound in their way as those of June 1789. Small groups of radical leaders came to the fore with the vigorous support of the populace. Their intention was to found a democratic republic that would express the revolutionary principles of unity, liberty, equality, and fraternity and would mobilize the nation to fight its enemies at home and abroad. To the democratic leaders, the constitutional regime was failing in these tasks because it represented the social hierarchy of those loyal to the monarchy rather than to the nation. And the monarchy seemed ready to betray the nation for the sake of ancient . . . links with foreign rulers. Accordingly, the new regime launched campaigns to destroy a wide range of enemies and suspects: monarchists, constitutionalists, members of the Feuillant Club, moderates, and [refractory] priests. The climate of fear, suspicion, and violent death created by the men of 10 August and their popular support was fundamentally different from the political climate of the constitutional monarchy. The republic continued to live, as it was born, by fear and violence. It succeeded in turning back the foreign armies and bringing victory out of defeat, but only at great cost. The liberal government, for which the men of 1789 had struggled, died a violent death."

Mobs attack the Palace of the Tuileries in an attempt to end the monarchy for all time.

Hordes of angry citizens enter the Palace of the Tuileries. The king's nine hundred Swiss guards were unable to fend off their attack.

no one to protect the king, Roederer urged the monarch and his family to take refuge in the Legislative Assembly at its meeting place in the Manège, just across the gardens. "Sire," pleaded Roederer, "Your Majesty has not five minutes to lose. . . . You do not have enough men to defend the [palace]."[54] The king hesitated: Should he give up and lay down his crown, or should he fight for it? Marie Antoinette wanted to fight, and she reminded Roederer that the palace was full of loyal, determined men. "Madame," replied Roederer solemnly, "all Paris is marching."[55]

Finally, the king consented to leave, and he and his family were escorted to the Manège. As the king walked across the gardens for the last time, he was heard to comment, "The leaves are falling early this year."[56]

Once inside the Manège, the group was placed in a small room reserved for reporters of assembly debates. The Feuillants and other deputies were absent, hav-

ing fled in fear from the mobs. Most would never return to their duties.

Meanwhile, a crowd of about twenty thousand citizens and *fédérés* armed with muskets, pikes, and pitchforks converged on the palace. The Swiss guard fought determinedly, but they were soon overwhelmed. Over five hundred guards lay dead as the mob stormed the building and slaughtered the remaining defenders and everyone else in the palace, even servants, cooks, and ushers. They looted treasures and destroyed furnishings. The violence continued throughout the day. In the evening sky, flames from the burning Tuileries could be seen across Paris.

The next day, the assembly, bowing to the power of the Insurrectionary Commune, voted to depose the king. The commune ordered the king and his family to be imprisoned in a gloomy building called the Temple. The once-great king of France was king no more, and the Revolution was now taking a new and fearful course.

Chapter

7 The End of Monarchy, the Beginning of Terror

France had no king. The Legislative Assembly had lost many of its members. The Paris Commune had been unlawfully dismissed. At last, those sympathetic to the common people held the power of the nation in their hands. But what would they do with it?

Over twelve hundred had been killed during the August 10 attack on the Tuileries. Many were innocent victims caught in the violence that spilled over into Paris streets. With the August 10 uprising, violence and terror became firmly entrenched as a political tool of the radical revolutionary leaders.

The Insurrectionary Commune was now running the country. It immediately appointed an executive council that would take over the power of the king and would rule in collaboration with the commune and municipal assemblies. The committee included the king's old Girondin ministers to whom was added one more—Georges Danton as minister of justice.

Danton was a rough-looking man, of medium height, broad, with bristling brows over a wide face disfigured by smallpox. His lips were scarred and thickened and his nose flattened as a result of being attacked by a bull as a child. By his appearance, one would never guess that he was the son of a middle-class lawyer,

well educated in the classics, able to read English and Italian, and a lawyer himself. Danton was a powerful speaker who used dramatic gestures to emphasize his thundering voice. He was boisterous, jovial, and well liked by the people, but he did not flinch at using the violence and brutality of the mob to his advantage. He seemed to fit more comfortably with the

Minister of Justice Georges Danton worked hard to unite the various revolutionary contingents. Well liked by the people, he also encouraged mob violence.

Danton with a Dagger

Georges Danton was a powerful leader in the events following the king's fall. Madame Roland was well acquainted with Danton, since her husband was on the executive council along with him. Although Danton was determined to further the Revolution, Madame Roland found him distasteful and untrustworthy. She describes her impressions of Danton, which are recorded in a translation by Evelyn Shuckburgh, The Memoirs of Madame Roland.

"Danton scarcely let a day go by without coming to see me. Sometimes it was for the Council; he would then arrive a little early and come to my apartment or he would stay behind after the meeting, usually accompanied by Fabre d'Eglantine. Sometimes he would invite himself to supper on a day when I was not normally receiving, in order to discuss some matter with Roland. No one could have shown more zeal, a greater love of Liberty or a stronger desire to agree with his colleagues in [Liberty's] service. I used to look at his repulsive features and although I told myself that one must not judge by appearances, that I knew nothing certain against him and that the most honest of men must be allowed two faces in a time of turmoil, I could not read into that face the image of an honest man. I have never seen features which reflected so clearly the licence of brutal passions; an astonishing audacity emanated from them, partly hidden by an air of vulgar joviality, an affectation of frankness. I have a lively imagination and when people impress me I tend to [imagine] them performing actions which suit their character. I can never look for any length of time at a [face] which is a little out of the ordinary without clothing the owner with the uniform of some profession or giving him a role which fits my idea of his nature. My imagination has often figured Danton with a dagger in his hand, inciting by voice and gesture a gang of assassins more timid or less ferocious than himself, exulting in his crimes and demonstrating his depraved inclinations."

rowdies of the Cordeliers than with the well-off Jacobin gentlemen. But despite his roughness and questionable tactics, he worked hard to unite the revolutionary leaders. Danton had achieved a powerful position—he not only had influence in the Insurrectionary Commune, which he had helped install, but he held a position on the new executive council that controlled the government as well.

Immediately following the uprising of August 10, royalist newspapers were suppressed, their printing presses given to the radical journalists such as Jean-Paul Marat.

A municipal watch committee was established that had the power to arrest anyone suspected of being royalist or counterrevolutionary.

Meanwhile, what was left of the assembly, all republican democrats, called for a new democratic national convention. Unlike previous elections of deputies to the assembly, the elections to the new convention would be democratic—people did not have to pay taxes or own land to vote. All men aged twenty-one or older could participate. (Although it was thought to be democratic, the vote was limited to men only; women were prevented from voting.) The first task of the convention would be to draw up a new constitution establishing a republican form of government—one in which there would be no king and in which the power would reside in the people and their elected representatives, not the head of state. Deputies to the new national convention would be elected within a few weeks and were scheduled to meet for the first time on September 21, 1792. The problems they would face would be enormous.

The September Massacres

On August 19, 1792, an army of Prussians, Austrians, and émigrés crossed the French frontier. By August 30, the French stronghold of Verdun, just two hundred miles from Paris, was under siege by the Duke of Brunswick's armies. He had earlier threatened to destroy Paris. If Verdun fell, the enemy would have an open road to Paris. At the same time, in the western province of Vendée, royalist citizens began protesting the Revolution.

Paris was in a state of terror. The assembly, announcing once again that the country was in peril, called for volunteers. The streets were filled with the sounds of marching boots, beating drums, and tearful goodbyes as young men went off to defend their country against foreign invaders. In the middle of all this frantic activity was Georges Danton, whose powerful speeches calmed the panic and gave the people a direction and a determination to overcome the threat. "Citizens," he declared, "no nation on earth has obtained liberty without a struggle. You have traitors in your bosom; well, without them the fight would have been soon over."[57] His speech not only encouraged the people, it raised the specter of "traitors within"—

Radical journalist Jean-Paul Marat played his part in encouraging the crowd to murder members of the Swiss guard and the clergy.

secret royalists, refractory priests, aristocrats, or agents of the enemy. Radical journalists such as Jean-Paul Marat already were not only declaiming the dangers of "traitors within," but even suggesting that good citizens "go to the Abbaye [a prison] . . . seize priests, and especially the officers of the Swiss guards and their accomplices and run a sword through them."[58] Placards bearing these inflammatory statements were posted throughout Paris. Widely circulated pamphlets and journals aroused the fears and hatred of aristocrats and counterrevolutionaries. With the very real threat of foreign invasion, people readily believed there were traitors among them. What would happen when all the able-bodied men had left Paris to fight the enemy armies? Were these traitors waiting for just this opportunity to rise up and slaughter the helpless women and children of Paris, as journalists suggested? The people, already frightened by their enemies besieging Verdun, were ready to believe in such a danger.

On September 2, 1792, news reached Paris that Verdun had fallen. At that very time, Danton was giving his most famous speech:

> The tocsin [alarm bell] that shall be sounded is not a signal of alarm but a summons to charge against the enemies of the *patrie*. To vanquish them, Messieurs, we need boldness, always boldness, and still more boldness and then France will be saved![59]

The events that began later on that day of September 2 are a subject of debate among historians. Were they planned in advance? Did Danton encourage them? Could anyone have stopped them? What is certain is that no one in the commune or assembly made an effort to halt the terrible massacres that began that sunny September afternoon.

It all started when several coaches carrying refractory priests on their way to the Abbaye prison were stopped, and the priests were dragged from the coaches and murdered. The mob, many of them the rough *fédérés* from Marseilles, then moved to the Carmes prison where they began murdering the 150 priests imprisoned there. Someone decided the prisoners should receive a "trial." Victims were brought to a mock trial and asked a few questions before being sent off to be butchered. The killings went on into the night. The mob lit bonfires so that they

Marie Antoinette's close friend Princess Lamballe is brought before the Revolutionary Tribunal.

could see to continue their bloody work. But by dawn, the work was not yet done. The killings in Paris went on for five days. In the end about fourteen hundred people were murdered. All but two Paris prisons were attacked. Most of the victims were men, but women and children were murdered, too. The Princess Lamballe, Marie Antoinette's close friend, was one of the victims. By September 7, the bloodbath had spent itself.

Victory at Valmy

Less than two weeks after the massacres, the French armies met their greatest challenge. At Valmy in the Argonne forest of France, the Prussian army led by Brunswick was turned back by French artillery and by masses of new French volunteers burning with patriotism. The famous poet-philosopher Johann Wolfgang von Goethe, who had accompanied the Prussian forces, was an eyewitness to the Prussian defeat.

> In the morning we had been talking of roasting and eating the French. . . . Now people avoided each other's eyes and the only words uttered were curses. In the gathering darkness we sat in a circle. We did not even have a fire as we usually had. Almost everyone remained silent . . . then someone asked me what I thought of the events of the day. . . . So I simply said, "At this place, on this day there has begun a new era in the history of the world; and you can all claim to have been present at its birth."[60]

On the very day that the French general Dumouriez was battling the Prussians,

Radical Jacobin Louis de Saint-Just pressed for the trial and execution of the king, arguing that no one could rule justly.

the deputies to the new National Convention were taking their seats for the first time.

Almost from the beginning there was bitter animosity between the two most influential groups at the convention, the Girondins, now a separate political force, and the Jacobins. Many of the deputies had sat on the old Legislative Assembly, but the newly elected deputies from Paris, who were in sympathy with the sansculotte, were to play an important role. The Paris delegation included the radical Jacobins Robespierre, Camille Desmoulins, and a hard, unpleasant young man named Louis de Saint-Just. The most radical members of the Paris delegation were Jean-Paul Marat and the journalist Hebert whose followers became known as *enragés* or "madmen." The Jacobins occupied the highest seats in the assembly hall, to the

Louis XVI pleads for his life during his trial on December 26, 1792.

left of the president's desk, and for that reason they became known as the Mountain. To the right of the president sat the Girondins, who generally represented the wealthy middle class and the interests of the provinces. In the center sat the largest group of deputies, who were not committed to either the Jacobin or Girondin points of view. Because of their central location in the hall in lower seating they were known as the Plain.

Despite their differences, all factions agreed on the first act of the convention: On September 21, the convention officially declared the monarchy abolished. King Louis XVI had been deposed; now the position of monarch itself was abolished. The convention also agreed that September 22, 1792, would be the first day of Year I of the Republic.

The agreement ended there. The Girondins quickly mounted an attack on their Jacobin opponents, blaming them for the September massacres, attacking the Insurrectionary Commune, and engaging in spiteful personal attacks on deputies of the

Mountain. Finally, Danton, who had attempted to bring the rival factions together, became disgusted with the Girondins, resigned from the executive council, and gave his support to the Mountain.

"I Die Innocent"

In November, a box containing the king's secret papers was found in the Tuileries. The papers included evidence sufficient to convict the king of treason. The Jacobins were delighted at the find. For months they had been calling for the trial and execution of the king, with Louis de Saint-Just leading the movement. "It is impossible," he had claimed, "to rule innocently."[61] Girondins had resisted the idea. But faced with such evidence, there was little they could do. In December 1792, the king was brought to trial. There was little doubt that he would be found guilty, but the Girondins still hoped to avert his execution. The Girondin leader Brissot came to his defense: "No republican will ever be brought to believe that . . . in order to destroy the office of King, the man who fills it must be killed."[62]

Nevertheless, the Jacobins, supported by the Parisian sansculotte, insisted on the death penalty. On January 21, 1793, Louis Capet, of the house of Bourbon, former king of France, was sent to the guillotine. As he mounted the scaffold steps, Louis motioned to the drummers to be silent. He began to address the crowd which had gathered. "I die innocent," he began, but his last words were cut off when the drummers hastily resumed their drum rolls. With a swish of the blade, Louis's head was severed. One of the guards picked it up to show to the crowd, and for a moment there was silence. Then the crowd began to shout, *"Vive la nation! Vive la république!"* Louis was buried in a plain coffin in a commoner's grave.

The king's execution shocked all of Europe. Regicide (the murder of a king) was a terrible crime in the eyes of other nations. European monarchs were already nervous at the National Convention's declaration in November 1792 that France would "extend fraternal feelings and aid to all peoples who may wish to regain their liberty."[63] In other words, France was promising to aid revolution in other nations. The governments of those nations were now determined to wage all-out war against France's revolutionary government.

Realizing the inevitability of conflict and encouraged by the French victories at Valmy, the National Convention declared war on England in February 1793, then on the Netherlands, and then on Spain. Already at war with Austria and Prussia, in the space of a few weeks France was at war with almost every major power on the continent.

A guard holds the king's severed head for the crowd to see. Moments later, thousands of citizens yelled triumphantly, "Vive la république!"

The King's Last Day

The king's young daughter, Madame Royale, was the only member of the royal family to survive the Revolution. Her memoirs were later published under the title Private Memoirs on the Captivity of the Royal Family in the Tower of the Temple. *Here she describes her family's reactions the night before Louis's execution.*

"The family learned the sentence on Sunday the 20th [January 1793] from the hawkers who came to cry it out under their windows, at seven in the evening. A Convention decree allowed the Princesses to descend to the King's room. They ran there and found him very changed; he was crying with anguish for them, and not for fear of death. . . . Then he gave excellent religious instruction to his son, enjoining him to pardon those who were sending him to his death, and he gave his blessing as well to his daughter. The Queen ardently desired that the whole family spend the night with Louis XVI; he refused, making her understand that he needed tranquillity. She requested that she be at least allowed to return the next morning—a request to which he assented. But when they were gone, he asked his guards not to permit them to come down again because that caused him too much pain."

After learning of his impending execution, the king's family members demand to see him to say goodbye.

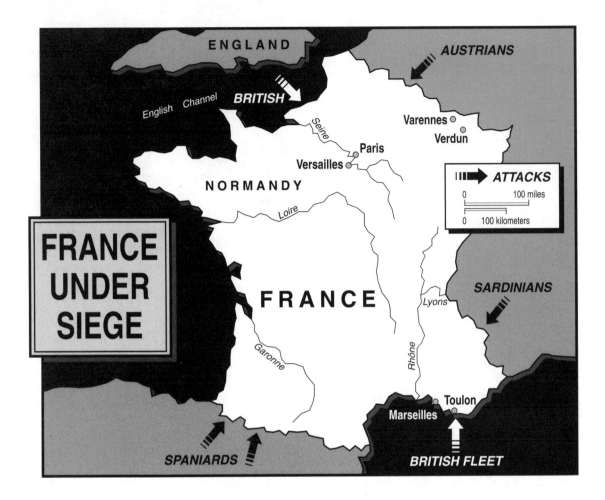

At first, the war seemed to go well. The Girondin general Dumouriez had not only pushed invading armies out of France but he had invaded other territories. As long as Dumouriez was successful, the popularity of the Girondins at home seemed assured.

The extended war soon began to tell on France. There were more coastlines and frontiers to guard. The threat of counter revolutionaries and royalist uprisings was still very real. The value of the assignats continued to fall while the cost of living rose. Food shortages became a problem again. Peasants and sansculotte were the first to feel the pinch and began to demand price controls.

In the spring of 1793, General Dumouriez met with a series of military defeats and was forced to withdraw. Disgusted with the ineffective government of the convention and the course the Revolution was taking, Dumouriez deserted to the Austrians. Dumouriez was identified with the Girondins, and his desertion marked the turning point in the Girondins' fortunes.

To make matters worse, violence had broken out in the conservative Catholic, royalist province of Vendée. To meet the new demands for troops when the war was extended, the convention needed three hundred thousand new recruits, and recruiting officials were sent to the provinces. Tens of thousands of angry peasants, unwilling to fight for a government to which they felt no loyalty, armed themselves with pikes and pitchforks. They massacred revolutionaries, scattered National Guard troops, and attempted to open a port for a British invasion fleet.

Given the defeat and defection of Dumouriez and the continuing economic problems that the Girondin leaders seemed unable to address, the moderates and uncommitted members of the Plain in the convention began to favor the Jacobins. With their new allies, Danton and other leaders were able to push through a series of emergency measures to meet the national crisis, some of which would have far-reaching effects. Émigrés who returned to France were to be executed. The newly established watch committees were to keep tabs on all foreigners, watching for any suspicious behavior. One of the most important measures was the establishment of the Revolutionary Tribunal or court whose job was to try those accused of counterrevolutionary activities. Danton defended the establishment of the tribunal: "Let us become terrible so that we can prevent the people from being terrible."[64] Finally, a Committee of Public Safety made up of convention deputies was established to act as a link between the executive council and the convention. From the beginning, the Mountain controlled the committee, whose first leader was Danton. The committee held its meetings in secret, and it quickly took over the powers of the ministers on the executive council.

Jean-Paul Marat escaped execution because of his immense popularity with the common people. In his writings, he was known for slander and untrue accusations.

The Fall of the Girondins

In the meantime, the sansculotte had been calling for the removal of the Girondins from the convention. They blamed the Girondins for trying to block the execution of the king, for refusing to pass price controls, and for the defection of Dumouriez. In his radical journal *The Friend of the People*, Jean-Paul Marat called for the arrest of the Girondins in the convention. Girondins responded by calling Marat before the Revolutionary Tribunal. But they had miscalculated his popularity.

Marat was an unlikely friend of the people. He was a small man with dark, stringy hair, green eyes, and a yellowish complexion. He wore tattered clothes and paid little attention to personal hygiene, despite a painful skin disease. His character matched his unclean appearance. In his writings, he seemed willing to attack or slander anyone, especially those in power, without concern for the truth. Even though most members of the convention, even his allies, found Marat distasteful, he was a hero to the people. An English visitor to Paris who heard Marat speak describes him:

> When Marat is in the tribune [speaker's box] he holds his head as high as he can, and endeavors to assume an air of dignity. . . . Amidst all the exclamations and signs of hatred and disgust which I have seen [shown toward] him, the look of [self-approval] which he wears is [amazing]. . . . He speaks in a hollow croaking voice, with affected solemnity, which in such a [small] figure would often produce laughter, were it not suppressed by horror at the character and sentiments of the man.[65]

Nevertheless, the people loved him. He was quickly acquitted, and the affair seemed to make him all the more popular.

By May of 1793, the struggle between the Girondins and the Mountain became bitter, but the Mountain clearly had momentum in its favor. In an effort to win the support of the sansculotte, the Mountain forced through the convention a decree allowing municipalities to set maximum prices on grain and flour and forcing suppliers to send grain to market.

In frustration, the Girondins turned on the Insurrectionary Commune. The *enragé* publisher Hebert, a member of the commune, was arrested, as were other radicals. This repressive act brought matters to a boiling point. At a speech given at the Jacobin Club, Robespierre called on the people to revolt:

> When all the laws are being violated, when despotism has reached its peak, and when good faith and decency are being trampled underfoot, it is then that the people must rise up. That moment has now arrived.[66]

In response, the sections of Paris set up an insurrectionary committee and organized an uprising. On Sunday, June 2, thousands of armed citizens and national guardsmen surrounded the hall where the National Convention was meeting. A delegation burst into the meeting hall demanding "justice against the guilty"—the arrest of the Girondin leaders. After discussion on how to handle the mob, the deputies decided to leave the hall.

Publisher Hebert, a member of the Paris Commune, was arrested with other radicals in May 1793.

In a final triumph, the Jacobins manage to defeat the Girondins, whose leaders are carted off to the scaffold to be executed.

However, once outside, the deputies found that they were surrounded by eighty thousand angry Parisians and national guardsmen. Having nowhere to go, they retreated to their meeting hall, where, after much debate, they passed a decree calling for the arrest of more than twenty Girondin leaders.

Thus, the struggle between the Girondins and the Jacobins, which had begun in the Legislative Assembly, was finished. But now the Jacobin-controlled Committee of Public Safety alone would have to answer the demands of the sans-culotte for bread and justice without provoking them. The Committee of Public Safety would have to find a way to subdue uprisings in the provinces and to defend the nation against hostile armies. At first the crises appeared beyond the control of the Jacobins. But for Maximilien Robespierre, the national crisis was the long-awaited opportunity for which he had prepared himself.

8 The Reign of Terror

Many Girondins had fled Paris to provinces that were sympathetic to their cause. There they stirred up rebellion against the Parisian government, a government that the provincials had always distrusted.

In addition to Girondin-led uprisings, the royalist uprising in the Vendée had become a full-scale civil war and had spread to other provinces. The most pressing problem, however, was the war: British, Austrian, and Spanish armies were threatening the frontiers.

Robespierre

The Committee of Public Safety, led by Danton, was unable to deal with the crisis. Finally, in July 1793, Danton was forced to resign from the committee, although he maintained his position as deputy in the convention. Maximilien Robespierre took his place on the Committee of Public Safety and soon would lead the Revolution to its next, most fearsome stage.

In another time in history, Maximilien Robespierre may have become what he had trained to be, a provincial lawyer practicing his profession in the town of Arras where he was born. But he was a young man in the middle of a great revolution, and Robespierre, more than most people, knew how to take advantage of the opportunities at hand.

Maximilien Robespierre's signature appears in the lower right corner of a Committee of Public Safety document from 1793.

Robespierre is viewed controversially by historians. Some see him as an incorruptible and tireless advocate for the people of France. Others see him as a vain and self-centered tyrant.

More than any other revolutionary leader, Robespierre has been the subject of controversy. Some historians see him as a great leader committed to the ideals of the Revolution and to bettering the lot of common people. Critics see him as ambitious, vain, self-centered, and more interested in achieving his own fame than in achieving liberty and equality for the people.

The Incorruptible

Robespierre was a small man with a thin pale face who wore an expression that his contemporaries described as catlike. His nasal voice was harsh and annoying, his style of speaking monotonous and academic, and his manner cold and aloof. He had no use for luxurious living, yet he was meticulous in his dress and appearance.

Long after they had gone out of style, he continued to wear the powdered wig and fancy clothes fashionable during the ancien régime. He favored the color green, and even wore green-tinted eyeglasses.

Robespierre had many acquaintances, but few friends, and yet he was widely admired, even by his enemies. Early in the Revolution the great leader Mirabeau recognized Robespierre's qualities, predicting "That man will go far; he believes what he says."[67] He was known by all as the Incorruptible, for he refused to be bribed or to make money from the Revolution.

Robespierre was devoted to the teachings of Jean-Jacques Rousseau, one of the leading philosophers of the Enlightenment, and he kept a copy of Rousseau's *Social Contract* by his bedside, much as people would keep a Bible. Robespierre was a champion of the common people and held a lofty, idealized notion of them as virtuous and noble, as Rousseau had taught. He genuinely believed in the common people's goodness, and he was able to make them feel that they were part of a noble, glorious cause. If they failed to live up to his ideal of them, he blamed the influence of foreign agents or their failure to follow his policies.

Despite his deeply held convictions, many of his contemporaries believed he was more interested in outward appearances, in fame, and in his own career than he was in the people. He was considered by many to be a hypocrite who loved himself far more than he loved the commoners. As evidence, his critics pointed to his overconcern with his physical appearance, and to his living quarters, which were filled with paintings, engravings, and a sculptured bust of himself. His critics claim that he was not interested in virtue for its own sake, but in being more virtuous than others. Nevertheless, Robespierre dedicated himself to the Revolution and he fervently defended the interests of the common people.

The Death of Marat

When Danton had led the Committee of Public Safety, he had attempted unsuccessfully to use diplomacy to end the war. Under Robespierre's leadership, the committee began to conduct the war vigorously against rebels at home and enemies abroad. However, the people wanted more. Radical groups demanded that the government put an end to hoarding and speculating in grain. They wanted the death penalty for hoarders, and they wanted the government to control the rapidly rising prices of butter, soap, and other necessities.

Their cause was helped along by the martyrdom of one of their most popular leaders, Jean-Paul Marat. As author of the newspaper *The Friend of the People* and deputy and member of the Mountain, Marat was considered a hero by the sansculotte. But he was seen as an enemy by others. One was a young countrywoman, Charlotte Corday, daughter of a poor but aristocratic family from the town of Caen in Normandy. She was a fervent supporter of the Girondins, and like them, an admirer of the philosopher Rousseau. When the Girondins were overthrown, she

In Defense of Commoners

Robespierre proved a champion of the common working people. In 1791, when the assembly deputies were debating the issue of granting the vote to all citizens, Robespierre was quick to come to the defense of commoners. In Leaders of the French Revolution, *editor J. M. Thompson quotes Robespierre's speech.*

"Do you really think that a hard and laborious life produces more vices than luxury, ease, and ambition? Have you really less confidence in the virtue of our laborers and artisans . . . than in that of tax-collectors, courtiers, and the so-called nobility? For my part, I bear witness to all those whom an instinctively noble and sensitive mind has made friends and lovers of equality, that in general there is no justice or goodness like that of the people, so long as they are not irritated by excessive oppression; that they are grateful for the smallest consideration shown to them, for the least good that is done to them, and even for the evil that is left undone; that in the poor, and under an exterior that we should call coarse, are found honest and upright souls, and a good sense and energy that one would seek long and in vain among a class that looks down upon them."

A fervent supporter of the Girondins, Charlotte Corday was determined to strike a blow against the sansculotte.

served as a writing table. She reminded him of the note she had sent him. He nodded and asked for more information. She began to give him names of counterrevolutionaries in her district, and he quickly scribbled them down. When finished, he smiled at her. "They will soon be guillotined," he exclaimed.[68] At those words, Charlotte Corday plunged her knife into his chest, piercing his heart. Then she turned and calmly walked out of the room. Marat called out for help, but before anyone could reach him he was dead. His murderess was stopped before she left the house, and a few days later was brought before the Revolutionary Tribunal, where she was condemned to the guillotine. "I condemned one man in order to save a hundred thousand," she told her accusers.[69]

With Marat's death, Robespierre was left as the sole leader of the Mountain, and on July 27, when he joined the Committee of Public Safety, he became the most powerful leader of the Revolution as well.

Corday murdered Marat with a knife while he soaked in a bath to ease the pain of his skin disease.

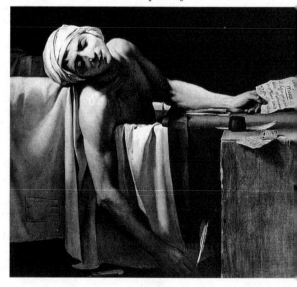

determined to strike a blow at the radical sansculotte by destroying one of their most popular leaders.

She went to see Marat at his home after sending a note that she had information about counterrevolutionaries. Before going to visit him, she had pinned a letter to her dress explaining her actions; she had also added her birth certificate, so there would be no doubt about her name. She carried a steel knife concealed in her skirts. After being turned away three times, she managed to gain admittance. Marat was soaking in a high-walled copper tub containing a mineral-salt bath to ease the pain of his crippling skin disease. His head was wrapped in vinegar-soaked cloths, and next to the tub was a rough board that

The assassinated Marat is removed from his room while Corday is led away.

"Let Terror Be the Order of the Day"

When the new convention had met in September 1792, they declared September 22, 1792, as the first day of Year I of the Republic. Under Girondin leadership, they began to draft a new republican constitution, but because of the feuds and divisions between Girondins and Jacobins, little headway was made. After the fall of the Girondins in June 1793, the Mountain quickly drafted its own more radical version of a constitution in hopes of appeasing the people. Under the new constitution, all adult males could vote, and the government would be responsible for seeing that everyone had a job and an education. However, the convention was unwilling to put the constitution into effect until the war and rebellions were under control. The convention wanted to maintain the emergency wartime powers it had proclaimed: the watch committees, the Revolutionary Tribunal, and the Committee of Public Safety, which originally had been established to serve as a link between the executive council of ministers and the convention. However, under Robespierre's leadership, the Committee of Public Safety gradually took over the executive powers of government.

The death of Marat had caused great anxiety; people believed it was part of a wider plot to overthrow the Revolution. Pressed by radical Hebertists, the committee began a stronger prosecution of the war against enemies within and without the country. Unsuccessful generals were brought before the Revolutionary Tribunal for treason and were executed. More troops were ordered into provinces to destroy the royalists and rebels. In August, the government issued an astonishing decree: the *levée en masse*. All citizens of France—men, women, children—were drafted to fight in the war effort.

A Portrait of Charlotte

Charlotte Corday (her full name was Marie-Anne-Charlotte Corday d'Armont) genuinely believed that by assassinating Marat she had done a heroic deed that would change the course of the Revolution. With that in mind, she wrote to her jailers a last request. Her letter is quoted in Last Letters: Prisons and Prisoners of the French Revolution 1793-1794, *by Olivier Blanc.*

"On 15 July 1793, Year II of the Republic.
To the citizens of the Committee of General Safety.

Since I have only a few moments left to live, might I hope, citizens, that you will allow me to have my portrait painted. I would like to leave this token of my memory to my friends. Indeed just as one cherishes the image of good citizens, curiosity sometimes seeks out those of great criminals, which serves to perpetuate horror at their crimes. If you [agree to grant] my request, I would ask you to send me tomorrow a painter of miniatures [small portraits]. . . . Believe, I beg you, in my sincere gratitude.

Marie Corday"

Her request was granted, and it was reported in a revolutionary newspaper of the day that the artist, Citizen Hauer, was seen at her trial drawing her portrait. She was pleased with his work which she found "well executed and a good likeness." *The newspaper reported that she posed for her portrait* "with unimaginable tranquillity and gaiety."

Charlotte Corday firmly believed that murdering Marat would save the lives of innocent people whom he accused of being traitors.

The Revolutionary Tribunal had the power to punish anyone suspected of counterrevolutionary activities.

Still the radicals were not appeased. A drought in the summer of 1793 brought on more bread shortages. And when news reached Paris that royalists had handed over the city of Toulon to British armies, people feared not only bread shortages but a widespread aristocratic plot. The people demanded that maximum prices be set on all goods and that suspects be arrested. The convention gave in to the demands, setting maximum prices and passing the Law of Suspects. This law allowed the Revolutionary Tribunal to punish anyone they found guilty of being an enemy of the Revolution. This condemned people who were relatives of émigrés, who spoke or wrote anything opposing the Revolution, or who showed sympathy for those being punished, even if they were relatives of the victim. The revolutionary watch committees were charged with seeking out these so-called suspects and bringing them before the tribunal. Thus the stage was set for the Jacobin Club's demand: "Let terror be the order of the day."

The Terror was conducted and controlled by the Committee of Public Safety, composed of twelve men. Their clear leader was Robespierre, who set the policies of the committee. Two members assisted him: the cruel young man, Louis de Saint-Just, who became known as the "Angel of Death," and the lawyer Georges Couthon.

Religion and Culture in the Republic

The Revolution had a profound effect beyond the government of France. It invaded every aspect of French life. Christianity was attacked by the radical republicans, who were anxious to do away with every trace of the ancien régime. Babies were no longer named after Christian saints, but were often named after heroes of ancient Rome. Since the calendar was based on Christianity—time was measured from the birth of Jesus Christ—a new calendar was developed. The year from September 22, 1792, to September 22, 1793, was Year I. The weeks were divided into ten days, and there were twelve months of three weeks or thirty days each. The five days left over at the end of the year were a time of festival known as *sans-culottides*. The months were renamed for natural seasonal occurrences. For example, April 20-May 19 was called *floréal*, the month of flowers; July 19-August 17 was *thermidor*, the month of heat.

In fashion, red, white, and blue became the rage, with the stiff, elaborate dresses of the ancien régime being replaced by simple, soft muslin dresses. The red cap of the sansculotte became a symbol of the Revolution and was worn by working class Parisian men. The elaborate hairstyles and powdered wigs of ancien régime days were replaced by natural, simple hairdos.

Even language was affected. It was no longer fashionable to address people as "madame" or "monsieur," terms that smacked of the old social hierarchy. Instead, in republican France, people addressed one another as "citizen" and "citizeness." The new forms of dress and speech were at first adopted out of patriotism. However, under the Terror, to misspeak and use "monsieur" could very well open one to the charge of being suspect under the new law.

A Central Fact of Life

During the Terror, the guillotine became a central fact of life. With black humor, French citizens adopted the guillotine shape as a popular ornament. Snuffboxes were embossed with little guillotines; ladies wore jeweled guillotine pins and earrings; even children had a guillotine

The Revolution had a profound impact on many aspects of French life, including the calendar, which was replaced with one that did not reflect Christianity.

game in which they lopped off the heads of their dolls. Meanwhile, the real guillotines were kept very busy indeed.

The Terror came into full force in October 1793, with the trial of Marie Antoinette. The Revolutionary Tribunal relied on flimsy evidence, rumors, and outright lies to convict the ex-queen, and she went to the guillotine on October 16, 1793, a tired, prematurely aged, white-haired woman who nevertheless was able to retain her dignity to the last. As she mounted the scaffold, she accidentally stepped on the executioner's foot. "Pardon, Monsieur," she exclaimed; four minutes later that executioner held up her head to show to the crowd.

In November, the Girondins who had been arrested the previous June were brought before the tribunal, quickly found guilty, and executed. Madame Roland was also executed. (Her husband, who had fled Paris, committed suicide when he heard of her death.) The Duke of Orléans, whose creation, the Palais Royal, had played such an important role in the Revolution, was another victim. Even the former mayor of Paris, Jean-Sylvan Bailly, was dragged from retirement in the country to face the guillotine.

The rhythm of the Terror became predictable. Every morning people were brought before the Revolutionary Tribunal (which had been divided into four courts to speed up their work). Every afternoon tumbrels, two-wheeled wooden carts, carried the condemned to the public square, renamed Place de la Révolution, where the guillotine did its bloody work. At first, aristocrats, refractory priests, and counterrevolutionaries faced

Marie Antoinette is executed on October 16, 1793, by order of the Revolutionary Tribunal.

the tribunal. Soon the arms of the committee reached out to pull in larger groups: hoarders of food, people who muttered against the committee members, the woman who had shed tears at seeing her husband guillotined—all guilty of disloyalty to the Revolution. Robespierre believed that virtue was necessary to his ideal revolutionary state. (Unselfish devotion to the nation was his first principle of virtue.) He thought that the nation's virtue could only be maintained through ruthless punishment of dissenters to the Revolution. His motto was "virtue, without which terror is disastrous, and terror, without which virtue is powerless."[70] Saint-Just listed in chilling terms the crimes against the Revolution punishable by the Terror:

> There are three sins against the republic: one is to be sorry for State prisoners; another is to be opposed to the rule of virtue; and the third is to be opposed to the Terror.[71]

Marie Antoinette manages to maintain a haughty dignity as she is led to the guillotine.

The watch committees, the eyes and ears of the Committee of Public Safety, did their work well, ferreting out suspects by the thousands. Soon the overloaded tribunal began to try prisoners in groups of up to fifty. Justice was abandoned, leaving only terror. In the provinces, especially where there had been royalist uprisings, bloody excesses were common. In Lyons, representatives of the Terror found the guillotine too inefficient: Several hundred prisoners were killed at once with cannon fire. In another province, two thousand were placed on barges in the middle of the river, and the barges were sunk. As the Terror reached its peak, there was a backlog of prisoners, and conditions in the prisons were crowded, filthy, and disease-ridden. Many died before being tried.

The Fall of Danton and the Hebertists

Robespierre was uneasy with the movement toward de-Christianization. While he had turned from Catholicism, he still believed in God and believed that a truly virtuous state would need some form of religion. Furthermore, he was becoming paranoid and becoming more isolated from the public. He began to suspect that both the Terror and de-Christianization, which the Hebertists actively supported, were part of a foreign plot to turn people against the Revolution. In the meantime, the war was going well for the French armies. The royalist uprisings had been crushed and foreign armies had been turned back by the French. The Terror seemed to be no longer necessary. Robespierre seemed ready for a change of heart.

In November 1793, Danton returned to Paris after a six-week stay at his country home. He had been appalled by the excessive killing, and he attacked the Hebertists and called upon the convention to relax the Terror.

Perhaps the Terror once served a useful purpose, but it should not hurt innocent people. No one wants to see a person treated as a criminal just be-

The Place de la Révolution, where public executions ordered by the Revolutionary Tribunal took place.

(Left) Danton and Desmoulins are led to the scaffold after having been accused of treason. In reality, they merely protested the massive bloodshed of the Reign of Terror. (Below) As Danton approaches the scaffold he predicts that the people will turn against Robespierre and his followers in less than three months—a prediction that would turn out to be deadly accurate.

cause he happens not to have enough revolutionary enthusiasm.[72]

Danton called for government to be "sparing of human blood." Finally, in December, the Committee of Clemency was established to review the charges against people in prison.

The Hebertists were quick to launch a counterattack, speaking out against Danton in the Jacobin Club, which they now controlled. Their defense was successful, and their supporters in the convention disbanded the Committee of Clemency.

Meanwhile, Robespierre, who was naturally suspicious, and who had always considered Danton a rival for fame, decided that Danton was plotting against him as well. He decided that he must get rid of both the Hebertists and Danton. Robespierre accused Hebert and his followers of being part of the foreign plot. In March 1794, Hebert and his friends were arrested and in less than two weeks faced the guillotine.

Danton and his friend Camille Desmoulins were the next to come under attack. Both felt some remorse for the part they had played in overthrowing the

Girondins. Desmoulins had cried at their execution and was heard to insult Robespierre as a "soul dried up and withered by self-adulation." Danton had made enemies of Saint-Just and Billaud-Varenne, both members of the Committee of Public Safety. On the night of March 30, an arrest order was issued for Danton. The verdict was already decided, and on April 3,

The Gentle Guillotine

Today the guillotine is a symbol of the horror of the Reign of Terror, but it was originally designed as a humane method of execution, as author Simon Schama explains in his book Citizens: A Chronicle of the French Revolution.

"In December 1789, Dr. Joseph-Ignace Guillotin, deputy of the National Assembly, had proposed a reform of capital punishment in keeping with the equal status accorded to all citizens by the Declaration of the Rights of Man. Instead of barbaric practices which degraded the spectators as much as the criminal, a method of surgical instantaneity was to be adopted. Not only would decapitation spare the prisoner [needless] pain, it would offer to common criminals the dignified execution hitherto reserved for the privileged orders. . . .

A rather beautiful [picture] made to illustrate the humanity of Guillotin's device suggests dignified serenity rather than macabre retribution. The setting is [the countryside] since the good doctor wanted the site of execution to be moved beyond town, away from what he thought was the primitive spectacle of the gutter mob. The action is stoical, perhaps even sentimental, since the executioner too has been transformed, from a brawny professional into a sensitive soul required to avert his eyes as he slashes the cord with his saber."

Danton and Desmoulins and their supporters were sent to the guillotine. Robespierre, once friend to both these men and godfather to the baby son of Desmoulins, remained unperturbed. Before he died, Danton predicted that "the people will tear my enemies to pieces within three months."[73] His prediction was chillingly accurate.

In June 1794, Robespierre staged a massive festival in the Champ de Mars that he hoped would win people over to his new religion—the Cult of the Supreme Being. Robespierre had been determined to establish a "republic of virtue" based on equality. He believed a national religion was necessary to support the virtues of civic-mindedness and modesty that he envisioned. He realized that a colorful festival was the best way to get the people's attention and support for this religion.

The same month that the Cult of the Supreme Being was introduced, a decree was passed that broadened the definitions of what was suspicious. The decree was known as the Law of 22 *Prairial* (the month of meadows). Prosecutors soon were working day and night drawing up lists of the accused destined for the guillotine. Prisons were again filled to overflowing with the doomed. Meanwhile, citizens lived in a constant state of dread, fearing their name might appear on the prosecutor's list for some chance comment or some long-forgotten misdeed.

French armies were winning glorious victories, recapturing French territory and pushing into Spain, the Netherlands, and Belgium. The Committee of Public Safety and the Reign of Terror were originally established to meet the military emergency. But the Revolution's enemies were quickly dissolving before the onslaught of the French armies.

In Paris, Robespierre was becoming more paranoid and less popular. Many people were angry at the loss of Danton and thought Robespierre had become a tyrannical dictator. They had had enough of blood.

Robespierre quickly sensed the change in the wind and decided to take the offensive. On July 26, 1794, he appeared before the convention to denounce what he called a newly discovered conspiracy and

to promise swift punishment to the traitors. In what he thought was a shrewd move, he refused to reveal names, but announced that he would return to the convention the next day to name the traitors.

His enemies knew full well that their names would be announced before the convention the following day, and they hastily made a plan. On the morning of July 27—on the republican calendar, the 10th day of *thermidor*, Year II—Robespierre appeared before the convention as promised, along with his allies Saint-Just and Couthon. He began to speak, but before he could reveal any names, he was pushed from the platform by a deputy. Hurriedly, one deputy after another denounced Robespierre, calling for his execution. Robespierre tried to speak over the noise, but lost his voice. "Danton's blood chokes him," cried one deputy.

Finally, Robespierre, along with Saint-Just and Couthon, was arrested. The radical Insurrectionary Commune attempted to support him, and succeeded in getting

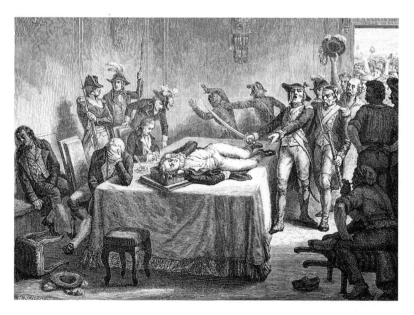

Robespierre lies wounded before the Revolutionary Tribunal, members of which believed him to have become increasingly paranoid and out of control.

The bloody Reign of Terror comes to an end with the execution of Robespierre and his fellow conspirators.

him freed, but they were not successful in mustering the support of the people. The sansculotte had no leaders left—Marat, Danton, Hebert, all were gone. The endless bloodletting had wearied the public, and there was no longer overwhelming support for the commune. Throughout the long night, Robespierre and his friends waited in the city hall. By early morning, six thousand men had been recruited by the convention to recapture Robespierre. As they burst into the city hall, Robespierre attempted to shoot himself but succeeded only in shattering his jaw. Robespierre and his party were taken to the offices of the committee in the Tuileries, where they waited for six hours while the convention debated their fate. All the while Robespierre's jaw was bound in a bloody bandage, and he was unable to speak. Finally, the group was taken to the Revolutionary Tribunal. By seven o'clock that evening they were carted off to the guillotine, as so many had been before them.

As Robespierre approached the guillotine, the executioner ripped the bandage off Robespierre's jaw. His screams of pain were quickly cut short by the thud of the blade.

And so Robespierre died. In the annals of the French Revolution, his name has become synonymous with the Reign of Terror. His critics have called him vain, ambitious, cruel, and hypocritical. But many years after his death, one of the few friends of his life wrote this of him:

> I would have given my life to save Robespierre, whom I loved like a brother. No one knows better than I do how sincere, disinterested, and absolute was his devotion to the Republic. He has become the scapegoat of the revolutionists; but he was the best man of them all. . . . It is fifty years since he died; but I still treasure in my heart the memory of him, and the lively affection which he inspired.[74]

9 The Final Years

The Terror was over. With the deaths of Robespierre and his followers, the French nation seemed to heave a great sigh of relief. Prisoners who would soon have met the guillotine under the Terror were released. (Among those released was Thomas Paine of American Revolution fame.) The Law of Suspects was repealed; the watch committees were disbanded. The power of the Committee of Public Safety was reduced, and the reorganized Revolutionary Tribunal acquitted many prisoners who would surely have met their death under the Terror.

A Swing to the Right

Political feeling swung to the right. The controls on prices and wages were lifted. Those officials most responsible for the Terror were tried and sentenced to the guillotine. Jacobin clubs were closed, and the remaining Girondins came out of hiding and returned to political life.

The leaders of the Parisian sansculotte had disappeared—some caught up in the Terror and some in the purge of the supporters of Robespierre that followed. In the spring of 1795, following a terrible winter in which many people starved or froze for lack of fuel, sansculotte twice attempted marches on the convention crying "Bread and the Constitution of 1793." They were easily turned away by the National Guard, now under the control of the convention.

Life had been grim under the Reign of Terror, with little joy in Paris, once the most glamorous city in Europe. With the end of the Terror, Paris once again was ablaze with gaiety as elegantly dressed men and women rode in elaborate carriages to theaters, restaurants, gaming rooms, and dance halls. Many bourgeoisie had become wealthy speculating in grain and other commodities, and they began to spend their new wealth extravagantly. The plain, modest styles and behavior of the Jacobin days were gone. Women wore low-cut, revealing dresses and elaborate hairdos; the private rooms of some theaters became notorious as "absolute sewers of debauchery and vice," according to a police report. Meals at expensive restaurants often cost as much as two months' worth of food for poor families. Parisians once again attended grand balls, many of which had a gruesomely humorous twist. These were called "balls of victims"; guests whose relatives had died in the Terror wore their hair piled high and a thin band of red ribbon around their necks, representing the mark of the guillotine.

Violence did not end, however, with the end of the Terror. Like a giant pendulum that swings back and forth, the end of leftist terror was followed by an almost equal and opposite reaction—a terror of the right. (The pendulum would swing back and forth again several times before coming to rest many years later.) A new group of ruffians took over the tactics of the Parisian sansculotte and became almost as feared. Called the *jeunesse dorée* or "gilded youth," these fashionably dressed and well-groomed young men were mostly middle class. No one would mistake them for bands of working class sansculotte, but like the sansculotte, they were intent upon violence. They carried short sticks

As Paris began to return to normal after the Reign of Terror, Parisians resumed their social activities. Here, a woman poses outside a Parisian theater.

weighted on the end with lead, which they used to attack leftist sympathizers or Jacobins and smash revolutionary symbols. Under their terror, the "red bonnet" of the sansculotte disappeared from the streets of Paris—no one dared wear it for fear of attack—and the Jacobin Club was vandalized and finally closed.

In some provinces there was an even stronger reaction, as people took vengeance against officials of the previous Reign of Terror. This new movement, known as the White Terror, was responsible for the deaths of hundreds who were massacred as mercilessly as the victims of the previous Terror had been.

Constitution of the Year III

Once the Reign of Terror was gone, France was adrift without a strong government. The convention, once dominated first by the Girondins and then by the Jacobin deputies of the Mountain, was now in the hands of moderates. They were responsible for maintaining the gains of the Revolution against royalist émigrés who were preparing to restore the ancien régime. They also wanted to keep the uprisings of the workers under control. Caught between these two opposing forces of left and right, delegates began drafting a new constitution—the Constitution of the Year III—which was passed on August 22, 1795, or according to the revolutionary calendar, the fifth day of *fructidor* (the month of fruit), Year III.

The new constitution established two chambers, or houses, of the legislature.

The executive power that once belonged to the king alone under absolute monarchy and to the Committee of Public Safety under the Reign of Terror was now placed in the hands of a group of five men called the Directory. Under the new constitution, the vote was once again limited to property owners. The deputies who now controlled the convention shied away from granting full equality to all citizens. As one deputy explained in justification of the new constitution:

> Absolute equality is [an impossibility]. If it existed one would have to assume complete equality in intelligence, virtue, physical strength, education and fortune in all men. . . . We must be ruled by the best citizens. And the best are the most learned and the most concerned in the maintenance of law and order. Now, with very few exceptions you will find such men only among those who own some property, and are thus attached to the land in which it lies, to the laws which protect it and to the public order which maintains it. . . . You must, therefore, guarantee the political rights of the well-to-do . . . and [deny] unreserved political rights to men without property.[75]

Despite its new look, the new government faced the same problems as the old:

threats from foreign powers, food short-ages, spiraling costs of living. (In the fall of 1795, the cost of living was nearly thirty times higher than it had been in 1790.) The new government would prove to be as ineffective at solving these problems as had the previous governments.

"A Whiff of Grapeshot"

Sensing that the new government was weak, royalists who wanted to restore the monarchy tried to stir up the Paris sections for an attack on the convention. The government turned to the army for help. With the able leadership of a young artillery officer named Napoléon Bonaparte, the crowd was turned back by what Napoléon later called "a whiff of grapeshot" from the cannons. The uprising in October 1795 would be the last that the streets of Paris would see for thirty years. The people, after five years of political struggle, lost interest in politics and turned to pleasure. As Bernard Mallet, great-grandson of the revolutionary journalist Mallet du Pan, wrote:

> Henceforth, when their will was being overruled by the Directory, when streets, bridges, and squares were bristling with troops and cannon, they went about their business or their pleasure [with unconcern]. . . . The Directory entered upon their rule with the immense advantage of a people to govern who [thought the safest course of action was to completely give up] political sentiment.[76]

In November 1795, after the Directory had held its first meeting, it announced its intentions:

When Napoléon Bonaparte became absolute ruler of France, the goals of the French Revolution seemed completely overturned.

> [To replace] the chaos which always accompanies revolutions by a new social order . . . [to] wage vigorous war on royalists, revive patriotism, sternly suppress all factions . . . destroy all desire for vengeance.[77]

The men of the Directory, all of mediocre talents, were ill equipped to carry out these good intentions. The country was in economic chaos. Royalists were plotting to reestablish monarchy; leftists wanted to overthrow the Directory. The rich were interested mainly in pleasure; the poor wanted bread.

The most extreme leftist position was best represented by a young journalist, François-Noël Babeuf. He called for common ownership of property and land and for the equal distribution of food supplies.

He insisted that only violence could establish this form of socialism, and so he and other conspirators began to recruit followers and make their plans. Babeuf and his coconspirators were soon discovered and arrested, then brought to trial. In May 1797, Babeuf and another conspirator were condemned to the guillotine.

Meanwhile, many of the new deputies to the legislature elected in April 1797 were constitutional monarchists who wanted a return of a king. The Directory felt that they had to remove the threat of monarchy once and for all. Once again they relied on the army. To do the job, Napoléon Bonaparte, now commander in chief of the army in Italy, sent home a rough, vulgar general named Pierre

Journalist François-Noël Babeuf called for major reforms in land ownership and the distribution of food and supplies. He was executed for his efforts.

Napoléon appointed Gen. Pierre Augereau to get rid of the remaining royalists after the French Revolution.

Augereau. "I have come here to kill the royalists," Augereau announced upon his arrival.[78] He commanded the coup d'état, or military takeover of the government, in which royalist deputies and officials were arrested and elections that had brought royalist deputies to power were annulled. The victory was complete, but a high price was paid—the government was becoming more dependent upon the army for its survival. And the government was becoming less trustworthy in the eyes of the people.

After successfully putting down the uprising in October 1795, Napoléon Bonaparte had quickly risen through the ranks. He successfully brought Italy under

French power. The Directors, realizing his popularity and his potential danger to them, were happy to have him out of the country. While Italy had been brought to heel by French armies, England was still threatening. And so, when Napoléon suggested an expedition to Egypt to thwart British shipping and set the stage for a

A Joyous Homecoming

After the fall of Robespierre and the Jacobins, there were many joyful reunions as people who had fled the country in fear of their lives returned to their homes and families. In her memoirs, Side Lights on the Reign of Terror, *the young Mademoiselle des Echerolles, who had been left in the care of friends, describes her experience.*

"The crisis which had ruined and killed so many worthy people seemed now to be settling into peace and conciliation. The Lyonnais émigrés were allowed to return to France, my father amongst them. . . . He sent me word of this happy state of affairs. . . . What a joy it was to receive this letter—promise of happiness and peace! I counted every day till my father's arrival; and then—I cannot describe my tears of joy when we met. . . . He described the dangers he had run in escaping to Switzerland; his anxiety about my fate. . . .

Our house in Moulins, which the Revolutionary Committee had occupied, was given back to us. . . . [Before leaving the house long ago, my aunt] had ordered all our silver plate to be hidden in one of the cellars. [Once at home] we were served by a Wallachian, a prisoner of war [named Joseph] . . . whom my father took as his domestic in order to remove him from the horrors of barrack life. . . . [Joseph and I] went down together into the small cellar where our treasure was hidden. It had not quite been emptied [by the Revolutionary Committee members] of the foreign wines with which we had filled it, but the greater part had been drunk; only a few stray bottles lay about on the ground, and were still piled in a heap over the very spot where we were now going to dig. We soon came upon the box . . . and Joseph, quite understanding that it had escaped the clutch of the Jacobins, who had so often entered this cellar, broke into cries of joy over every object he found, convinced that with each he obtained a fresh victory over 'these brigands, these thieves.'"

Napoléon forces the Directory to resign in 1799 as he becomes France's new military dictator.

French empire in the East, the Directors were all too happy to agree. In May 1798, the expedition embarked. At first it met with success. The news of pyramids and sphinxes inspired the people at home. Even more dazzling was the French discovery of the Rosetta stone, which allowed Europeans to decipher the Egyptian hieroglyphics. Despite its successes, however, the expedition was soon in trouble when the British fleet destroyed all but two French ships. Other nations became alarmed at French power and turned against France. Meanwhile, French armies in Germany and Italy suffered defeats.

The Directors' response to the crisis was to declare a general draft. Taxes were raised, but the economy was still in trouble. Discontent with the government was growing, and the Directors were under constant attack.

Realizing that there was no more glory to be won in Egypt, Napoléon handed over his command to a subordinate and sailed home, declaring "I am going home to drive out the lawyers."[79]

At home, the Abbé Sièyes, who had played a central role early in the Revolution with his pamphlet *What Is the Third Estate?*, was back on center stage. The political pendulum had swung back to the left, and Jacobins had made a resurgence. The bourgeoisie, who had gained so much in the Revolution, feared that Jacobin

The Dance Craze

When the Reign of Terror ended, all Paris began to dance. It seemed that citizens, especially young people, were trying to make up for their joylessness under the Terror overnight. In Daily Life in the French Revolution, *author Jean Robiquet describes the dance craze that took control of Paris.*

"[People thronged to restaurants and theaters.] But there was one passion which surpassed all others: dancing.

Within a few weeks, scores and then hundreds of dancehalls opened all over Paris. . . . There was not one deserted garden, not one abandoned dwelling, not one convent emptied of its nuns that was not dedicated [as a dancehall]. . . . [People danced] in half-ruined chapels and even on the worn flagstones of cloisters.

Organizers of this type of pleasure set up dancehalls to fit all purses. There was one where the admission fee was so low that 'even servants can go in.' Others are fitted out in greatest luxury for the sort of young ladies you might expect in such places, while others, more decent, were for honest bourgeois families looking for husbands for their daughters. . . .

Every evening, as soon as eight had chimed, the streets were filled with women in white going off to dance with their gallants. One of the most curious features of this universal passion was that it was spiced frequently with macabre associations. They danced on the souvenir of the guillotine, as they danced six years before on the ruins of the Bastille. Perhaps a certain amount of exaggeration crept into the tales of those famous Victims' Dances . . . where only authentic parents of those executed by the guillotine were admitted. On the other hand, the Victim Mood was within the reach of all women and a good number of them never went out without a death-pale face and a blood-red ribbon round the neck, marking the place were the guillotine fell. It was one way, among many others just as macabre, of brightening up Parisian night-life."

influence would endanger property rights or that Jacobins would once again call for full equality. They were ready for a strong leader who would consolidate the gains of the Revolution and bring a stable government. Sièyes believed he could be that strong leader, and he was looking for a strong general who could help him achieve power. His first choices were either unable or unwilling to serve. Finally, Sièyes approached Napoléon Bonaparte with the idea of taking over the government.

In many ways, Napoléon was a likely candidate. Even though he had met with little military success in Egypt, he was greeted as a conquering hero. He marched into Paris in splendid triumph, surrounded by cheering crowds. He knew that his moment had come, that France was at his feet. Earlier he had declared that the French "need glory, the satisfaction of their vanity; but as for liberty, they know nothing about it. . . . The nation needs a leader, a leader made illustrious by glory."[80]

The plot was laid, and the conspirators took control of the government by force of arms. On November 19, 1799—19 *brumaire* (the month of fog), Year VIII—the deputies of the two councils named Abbé Sièyes, Roger Ducos, and Napoléon Bonaparte as consuls. The three men were to take over the executive powers of the government. Napoléon was soon named first consul, and the other two quickly faded into the background. As Maximilien Robespierre had long before feared, the ten years of the French Revolution ended with a military dictator.

The Legacy of the Revolution

When the late premier of China, Chou En-lai, was asked about the significance of the French Revolution, he supposedly answered, "It's too soon to tell."[81] An exaggeration perhaps, for despite the bloody excesses and failures of the Revolution and the final victory of Napoléon, the revolutionaries made some important changes.

In some respects, peasants were no better off: The poor and landless could not vote and the majority could not afford to own land. On the other hand, some of the confiscated lands of the nobility and the church were purchased by peasantry. And peasants, while still bearing a heavy burden of taxes under the Napoleonic regime, no longer owed dues to a feudal landlord.

A symbolic image of the Revolution declares the goals of liberty, equality, and fraternity.

Robespierre's Cult of the Supreme Being was very short-lived, and the church was ultimately restored to a central place in French society. However, church property—which had accounted for 10 percent of French land under the ancien régime—was not restored, and the church never again exerted the influence with the state or with the common people that it had before the Revolution.

The bourgeoisie were the group who gained the most from the Revolution. Power in French society was no longer concentrated in the nobility but in business and professional people—the owners of property and money. Entry into this new aristocracy of wealth was determined by individual achievement, not birth.

Some of the revolutionaries' practical achievements lasted. Although the republican calendar, with its ten-day weeks and months named for events in nature, did not survive, another innovation of the National Convention—a metric system of weights and measures—not only survived but spread throughout the world.

Perhaps the most lasting legacy of the Revolution is its ideals, which still echo around the world today—"Liberty, Equality, Fraternity."

The men and women of the Revolution often backed away from the full realization of these ideals. Nevertheless, since the beginning of the nineteenth century, citizens of the world have invoked liberty, equality, and fraternity in striving to free themselves of tyrants, to achieve their full equal rights, and to work with others in their own nation and in other nations to achieve freedom and justice for all.

Notes

Introduction: The Best of Times, the Worst of Times

1. Albert Soboul, *The French Revolution 1787-1799*. Translated by Alan Forrest and Colin Jones. New York: Random House, 1974.
2. Norman Hampson, *The French Revolution: A Concise History*. New York: Charles Scribner's Sons, 1975.

Chapter 1: Roots of Revolution

3. Christopher Hibbert, *The Days of the French Revolution*. New York: William Morrow, 1980.
4. Quoted in Hibbert, *The Days of the French Revolution*.
5. J. Mills Whitham, *A Biographical History of the French Revolution*. 1931. Reprinted Freeport, NY: Books for Libraries Press, 1968.
6. Charles Downer Hazen, *Contemporary American Opinion of the French Revolution*. 1897. Reprinted Gloucester, MA: Peter Smith, 1964.
7. Hibbert, *The Days of the French Revolution*.
8. Whitham, *A Biographical History of the French Revolution*.
9. Whitham, *A Biographical History of the French Revolution*.
10. Quoted in Marilyn Yalom, *Blood Sisters: The French Revolution in Women's Memory*. New York: Basic Books, 1993.
11. Quoted in Hibbert, *The Days of the French Revolution*.

Chapter 2: A Gathering Storm

12. Quoted in Vincent Cronin, *Louis and Antoinette*. New York: William Morrow, 1975.
13. Quoted in Hibbert, *The Days of the French Revolution*.
14. Quoted in Cronin, *Louis and Antoinette*.
15. Quoted in Hibbert, *The Days of the French Revolution*.
16. Quoted in Simon Schama, *Citizens: A Chronicle of the French Revolution*. New York: Alfred A. Knopf, 1989.
17. Albert Soboul, *The French Revolution 1787-1799*.

Chapter 3: The Revolution Begins

18. Quoted in Hibbert, *The Days of the French Revolution*.
19. Quoted in George Rude, *The French Revolution*. New York: Weidenfeld & Nicolson, 1988.
20. Quoted in Hibbert, *The Days of the French Revolution*.
21. Quoted in Hibbert, *The Days of the French Revolution*.
22. Quoted in Yalom, *Blood Sisters*.
23. Quoted in Hibbert, *The Days of the French Revolution*.
24. Quoted in Hibbert, *The Days of the French Revolution*.
25. Soboul, *The French Revolution 1787-1799*.
26. Quoted in Soboul, *The French Revolution 1787-1799*.
27. Quoted in Hibbert, *The Days of the French Revolution*.
28. Quoted in Hibbert, *The Days of the French Revolution*.

Chapter 4: Bastille and the Summer of Violence

29. Quoted in Schama, *Citizens*.
30. Quoted in Cronin, *Louis and Antoinette*.
31. Quoted in Cronin, *Louis and Antoinette*.
32. Quoted in Schama, *Citizens*.
33. Quoted in Hibbert, *The Days of the French Revolution*.

34. Quoted in Yalom, *Blood Sisters.*

35. Quoted in Hibbert, *The Days of the French Revolution.*

36. Quoted in Hibbert, *The Days of the French Revolution.*

37. Quoted in Soboul, *The French Revolution 1787-1799.*

38. Quoted in Hibbert, *The Days of the French Revolution.*

39. Quoted in Hibbert, *The Days of the French Revolution.*

40. Quoted in Yalom, *Blood Sisters.*

Chapter 5: Making a New Nation

41. J. M. Thompson, ed., *English Witnesses of the French Revolution.* Oxford: Basil Blackwell, 1938.

42. Quoted in Hibbert, *The Days of the French Revolution.*

43. Quoted in Hibbert, *The Days of the French Revolution.*

44. Schama, *Citizens.*

45. Quoted in Soboul, *The French Revolution 1787-1799.*

46. Quoted in Yalom, *Blood Sisters.*

47. Quoted in Soboul, *The French Revolution 1787-1799.*

Chapter 6: The Widening War and the New Revolution

48. Quoted in Soboul, *The French Revolution 1787-1799.*

49. Quoted in Yalom, *Blood Sisters.*

50. Quoted in J. F. Bosher, *The French Revolution.* New York: W. W. Norton, 1988.

51. Quoted in Hibbert, *The Days of the French Revolution.*

52. Quoted in Hibbert, *The Days of the French Revolution.*

53. Quoted in Soboul, *The French Revolution 1787-1799.*

54. Quoted in David P. Jordan, *The King's Trial: Louis XVI vs. the French Revolution.* Berkeley: University of California Press, 1979.

55. Quoted in Jordan, *The King's Trial.*

56. Quoted in Jordan, *The King's Trial.*

Chapter 7: The End of Monarchy, the Beginning of Terror

57. Quoted in Schama, *Citizens.*

58. Quoted in Schama, *Citizens.*

59. Quoted in Schama, *Citizens.*

60. Quoted in Hibbert, *The Days of the French Revolution.*

61. Quoted in Cronin, *Louis and Antoinette.*

62. Quoted in Hibbert, *The Days of the French Revolution.*

63. Quoted in Soboul, *The French Revolution 1787-1799.*

64. Quoted in Hibbert, *The Days of the French Revolution.*

65. Thompson, *English Witnesses of the French Revolution.*

66. Quoted in Soboul, *The French Revolution 1787-1799.*

Chapter 8: The Reign of Terror

67. Quoted in J. M. Thompson, *Leaders of the French Revolution.* 1929. Reprinted Oxford: Basil Blackwell & Mott Ltd., 1962.

68. Quoted in *Horizon* eds., *The French Revolution.* New York: American Heritage Publishing, 1965.

69. Quoted in *Horizon, The French Revolution.*

70. Quoted in Thompson, *Leaders of the French Revolution.*

71. Quoted in Thompson, *Leaders of the French Revolution.*

72. Quoted in Hibbert, *The Days of the French Revolution.*

73. Quoted in Hibbert, *The Days of the French Revolution.*

74. Quoted in Thompson, *Leaders of the French Revolution*.

Chapter 9: The Final Years

75. Quoted in Hibbert, *The Days of the French Revolution*.

76. Bernard Mallet, *Mallet du Pan and the French Revolution*. London: Longmans, Green, 1902.

77. Quoted in Hibbert, *The Days of the French Revolution*.

78. Quoted in Hibbert, *The Days of the French Revolution*.

79. Quoted in Hibbert, *The Days of the French Revolution*.

80. Quoted in Leo Gershoy, *The French Revolution and Napoleon*. New York: Appleton-Century-Crofts, 1964.

Epilogue: The Legacy of the Revolution

81. Quoted in Schama, *Citizens*.

For Further Reading

Clifford Lindsey Alderman, *Liberty, Equality, Fraternity: The Story of the French Revolution*. New York: Julian Messner, 1965. A dramatic, historically accurate account of key events of the French Revolution.

Susan Banfield, *The Rights of Man, the Reign of Terror*. New York: J.B. Lippincott, 1989. A colorful, dramatic account of the events of the Revolution.

Alice Birkhead, *The Story of the French Revolution*. London: George G. Harrap, 1917. An older, quaint style, but a readable, colorful, dramatic account of the Revolution.

Horizon, eds., *The French Revolution*. New York: American Heritage Publishing, 1965. A concise and colorful account of the Revolution, beautifully illustrated with a wide range of art, cartoons, and pictures of documents and artifacts of the period.

M. and G. Huisman, *Stories of the French Revolution*. Translated by Barbara Whelpton. Cleveland, OH: World Publishing, 1966. Dramatic stories of events of the Revolution, including the story of the storming of the Bastille, the anthem *The Marseillaise*, and others.

Works Consulted

Marie Clothilde Balfour, trans., *Side Lights on the Reign of Terror: Being the Memoirs of Mademoiselle des Echerolles*. London and New York: John Lane, 1900. The personal account of Alexandrine des Echerolles, who was thirteen years old at the beginning of the Revolution, and who was forced to go into hiding with her family, who were royalists.

Olivier Blanc, *Last Letters: Prisons and Prisoners of the French Revolution*. Translated by Alan Sheridan. New York: Farrar, Straus and Giroux, 1987. A compilation of last letters written by the condemned under the Terror.

J.F. Bosher, *The French Revolution*. New York: W. W. Norton, 1988. A new interpretation of the Revolution that looks at the interplay of social forces.

Edmund Burke and Thomas Paine, *Two Classics of the French Revolution: Reflections on the Revolution in France and The Rights of Man*. New York: Anchor Books, Doubleday, 1989. *Reflections* is English statesman Edmund Burke's condemnation of the Revolution, and *The Rights of Man* is Thomas Paine's passionate rebuttal of Burke.

John Laurence Carr, *Robespierre*. New York: St. Martin's Press, 1972. A balanced view of one of the most complex, and perhaps most misunderstood, figures of the French Revolution.

Vincent Cronin, *Louis and Antoinette*. New York: William Morrow, 1975. A biography of the royal couple beginning with their youthful marriage and ending with the execution of the queen.

Rupert Furneaux, *The Last Days of Marie Antoinette and Louis XVI*. New York: John Day, 1971. A dramatic narrative of the fall of the French monarchy, beginning with the attack on the Tuileries on August 10, 1792. Includes many quotes from primary sources and a description of the fate of the royal children.

Leo Gershoy, *The French Revolution and Napoleon*. New York: Appleton-Century-Crofts, 1964. A scholarly analysis of the Revolution and the Napoleonic era. Includes an extensive annotated bibliography.

Norman Hampson, *The French Revolution: A Concise History*. New York: Charles Scribner's Sons, 1975. An overview of the salient events of the Revolution and their significance.

Charles Downer Hazen, *Contemporary American Opinion of the French Revolution*. 1897. Reprinted Gloucester, MA: Peter Smith, 1964. An analysis of the writings of Americans contemporary with the French Revolution, recounting their opinions about the Revolution.

Christopher Hibbert, *The Days of the French Revolution*. New York: William Morrow, 1980. In this retelling of the French Revolution, each chapter dramatizes events of the most momentous days of the Revolution, from the Bastille through Napoléon's coup.

David P. Jordan, *The King's Trial: Louis XVI vs. the French Revolution*. Berkeley: University of California Press, 1979. A detailed, readable narrative of one of the most extraordinary trials in the history of France.

Alex Karmel, *Guillotine in the Wings*. New York: McGraw-Hill, 1972. An analysis of the French Revolution and its relevance to contemporary America.

Georges Lefebvre, *The Coming of the French Revolution*. Translated by R. R. Palmer. 1947. Reprinted Princeton, NJ: Princeton University Press, 1989. Classic study of the early years of the Revolution.

————— *The Directory*. Translated by Robert Baldick. New York: Vintage Books, 1967. A detailed study of the government known as the Directory and events following the death of Robespierre up to Napoléon's coup d'état in 1799.

————— *The Great Fear of 1789*. Translated by Joan White, New York: Pantheon Books, 1973. Classic study by the noted French historian of the movement of panic and revolt that raged through France during the summer of 1789.

Bernard Mallet, *Mallet du Pan and the French Revolution*. London: Longmans, Green, 1902. A biography of the journalist Mallet du Pan, eyewitness and recorder of events of the Revolution, written by his great-grandson.

Gita May, *Madame Roland and the Age of Revolution*. New York: Columbia University Press, 1970. A rounded view of Madame Roland, a revolutionary idealist and one of the most complex, controversial, and interesting women of the Revolution.

Gouverneur Morris, *A Diary of the French Revolution, 1789-1793*, Vol I and Vol II. Edited by Beatrix Calry Davenport. Boston: Houghton, 1939. Diary entries and letters of this American minister to France during the Revolution, recording impressions of the French Revolution.

Jean Robiquet, *Daily Life in the French Revolution*. Translated by James Kirkup. New York: Macmillan, 1965. Glimpses of life in France from 1789 through the end of the Terror.

George Rude, *The French Revolution*. New York: Weidenfeld & Nicolson, 1988. A distinguished historian's definitive analysis of this complex event and how its effects continue as a vital force today.

Simon Schama, *Citizens: A Chronicle of the French Revolution*. New York: Alfred A. Knopf, 1989. An account of the Revolution focusing on the transformation of "subjects" to "citizens" and the role of the infatuation with modernity in creating the new order.

Evelyn Shuckburgh, trans., *The Memoirs of Madame Roland: A Heroine of the French Revolution*. Mount Kisco, NY: Moyer Bell Limited, 1989. Personal memoirs written from the Abbaye prison where Manon Roland, wife of a Girondin minister, spent the last months of her life before her execution under the Terror. The memoirs offer insights into events and personalities of the Revolution and into the character of this remarkable woman whom some critics describe as vain and self-serving and others consider a great heroine of the Revolution.

Albert Soboul, *The French Revolution 1787-1799*. Translated by Alan Forrest and Colin Jones. New York: Random House, 1974. Analysis of the events of the Revolution, focusing on the social and economic processes of the time.

J. M. Thompson, *Leaders of the French Revolution*. 1929. Reprinted Oxford: Basil Blackwell & Mott Ltd., 1962. This classic volume contains biographies of eleven of the outstanding leaders of the French Revolution, from the Abbé Sièyes to Maximilien Robespierre.

J. M. Thompson, ed., *English Witnesses of the French Revolution*. Oxford: Basil Blackwell, 1938. A collection of letters and diary entries by English citizens in France during the Revolution, recounting their impressions of events.

J. Mills Whitham, *A Biographical History of the French Revolution*. 1931. Reprinted Freeport, NY: Books for Libraries Press, reprinted 1968. Studies of the outstanding figures of the French Revolution and the key roles they played.

Marilyn Yalom, *Blood Sisters: The French Revolution in Women's Memory*. New York: Basic Books, 1993. Accounts written by women who witnessed the French Revolution, including those of the governess of the royal children, the servant of Marie Antoinette, and a peasant woman who fought as a soldier.

Index

Roman Catholic Church
  anger against leaders of, 20
  discouragement of free
    inquiry by, 22
  as dominant religion in
    France, 15
  obligations of peasants to, 11,
    20
  power of, 20
  reforming the, 60-62
  restored to influence, 113
  tithes to, 20
Rosetta stone, 109
Rousseau, Jean-Jacques
  Robespierre and, 90
  social contract of, 21, 23
Royale, Madame, 84
royalists, 56, 68, 106
  Directory's purge of, 107
  in the Vendée, 79, 85-86
royalty
  privileges of, 16, 18
Rude, George, 26
Russia, 63

de Saint-Just, Louis, 81, 82, 99
  arrest and execution of,
    101-102
  as assistant to Robespierre, 95
  the Terror and, 97
salt tax. See gabelle,
sans-culottides, 96
sansculottes, 49, 58, 65
  attack on Girondins, 86-88
  disappearance of, 103
  fear of, 66
  humiliation of king, 71-72
  Insurrectionary Commune
    and, 74
  National Guard and, 73
  rift between middle class and,
    66
Schama, Simon, 100
September massacres, 10, 79-81,
  82
Seven Years' War, 13
Shuckburgh, Evelyn, 78
Side Lights on the Reign of Terror

(des Echerolles), 108
Sièyes, Abbé Emmanuel-Joseph,
  56
  19 brumaire plot of, 109-111
  role of Third Estate and,
    31-33, 37-38
Soboul, Albert, 29, 37
Social Contract (Rousseau), 90
socialism, 106-107
Spain, 63, 101
  declaration of war on, 83
de Staël, Madame, 35, 48
Sun King. See Louis XIV
Swiss guards, 45, 74, 76

taille, the, 18, 24
de Talleyrand-Périgord, Charles-
  Maurice, bishop of Autun,
  60-61
taxes
  attempts to reform, 26-28
  Estates General and, 33
  exemptions from, 16, 18, 20,
    21, 24, 33
  peasants and, 17, 112
  under Louis XIV, 13
  under Napoléon, 112
  voting and, 59, 65, 73, 79
Temple, the, 76
Tennis Court Oath, 39-40
Terror, the
  Committee of Public Safety
    and, 95
  in full force, 96-102
  rightist reaction to, 104
Thompson, J.M., 19, 36, 53, 67,
  91
tithe, 20, 34
de Tocqueville, Alexis, 24
Toulon, 95
de Tourzel, Madame, 61, 65
transports militaires, 24
tricolor, 47-48, 52, 60, 96
Tuileries, 41, 55, 56, 63, 74, 82
  looting of, 76
Turgot, Anne-Robert, 25

unemployment, 29, 42, 48

Valmy
  victory at, 81, 84
Varennes
  flight of royal family to, 63-65
Vendée
  royalist uprising in the, 79,
    85-86, 89
Verdun, 79-80
Versailles, 12, 18, 23
  convening of Estates General
    at, 30, 34-35
  departure of royal family
    from, 52-55
  meeting of Assembly of
    Notables at, 27
de Voltaire, François-Marie
  Arouet, 22, 25

war
  causes of, 68
  Committee and progress of,
    98, 101
  Directorate and waging of,
    108-109
  disastrous beginning of, 70
  extension of, 83, 85-86
  Girondin agitation for, 69-70
  as prosecuted by Robespierre,
    93
  worsening of, 73
watch committees, 95, 98, 103
What Is the Third Estate? (Sièyes),
  32-33
White Terror, 104
workers, urban
  as members of Third Estate,
    16
  social hierarchy and, 17
  see also sansculotte

Yalom, Marilyn, 48, 50, 61
Young, Arthur
  France observed by, 18-19
  on hearing Sièyes speak, 32
  on pamphleteering in Paris,
    36
  on power of Jacobins, 57-58

Picture Credits

Cover photo: Giraudon/Art Resource, NY

Alinari-Scala/Art Resource, NY, 92 (top)

Archiv für Kunst und Geschichte, Berlin, 18 (bottom), 40, 49 (both), 75, 112

The Bettmann Archive, 10, 11, 12, 15 (bottom), 17 (both), 18 (top), 19, 23 (both), 25, 27, 28, 30, 32, 35, 36, 38, 44, 47 (bottom), 54, 58 (left), 64, 69, 80, 82, 83, 86, 87, 88, 89, 92 (bottom), 94, 99 (bottom), 101, 102

Bildarchiv Foto Marburg/Art Resource, NY, 41

Culver Pictures, 62, 65, 79

Giraudon/Art Resource, NY, 13, 16, 21, 31, 45 (both), 47 (top), 51, 58 (right), 59, 60, 66, 76, 77, 93, 96, 99 (top), 107 (top)

Erich Lessing/Art Resource, NY, 43, 98

Library of Congress, 106, 109

North Wind Picture Archives, 15 (top), 52

Snark/Art Resource, NY, 72, 81, 95, 97 (top), 107 (bottom)

Stock Montage, Inc., 34, 104

UPI/Bettmann, 70

About the Author

Phyllis Corzine received her B.A. in literature and language from Webster University in St. Louis and her M.A. in English and American literature from Washington University, St. Louis. She worked as an editor of educational materials for elementary and high school students for five years.

For the past four years she has taught English and worked as a freelance writer. Her work includes a variety of educational materials, as well as an adventure novel for young adults.

Corzine lives in St. Louis, and she has three children and two grandchildren. In her spare time she enjoys reading and gardening.